£9.99

NORLAND

NORLAND

The Story of
THE FIRST
ONE HUNDRED YEARS

· 1892 - 1992 ·

Researched and written by
PENELOPE STOKES

First published 1992
© Penelope Stokes 1992
ISBN 0 9517843 0 7

Published by The Norland College
Denford Park, Hungerford, Berks. RG17 0PQ
Designed by Brian Roll
Printed in Great Britain by
Abbey Press Raceview Business Park
Newbury Berks RG14 5SA

Dedication

This book is dedicated, with love, to the memory of Mrs. Emily Ward and to all those children and parents round the world and across the years who have been the beneficiaries of her selfless energy and far-sighted, radical thinking on child care personified by the 'Norlander'.

The Norland College
June 1992

ACKNOWLEDGEMENT

Much of the information for this history came from the comprehensive archives held by The Norland College. The author would, however, like to thank the following for their help:

Lady Atkinson, long-serving Director and Chairman of the Board from 1954 to 1984.
Bognor Regis Public Library.
Dr. John Burkinshaw, paediatrician, a resident of the Norland Nurseries from 1915 to 1923, and later a Director of the Institute.
Mr. Douglas Clarke, Director from 1937, Chairman from 1969 to 1981, and now Life President of the College.
Mrs. Dorothy Fawkes, Norland Tutor from 1969 to 1987 and Vice Principal, from 1987-1988.
Mrs. Sylvia Garnsey, Head Mistress of Norland Place School.
The Mansell Collection, for permission to reproduce the photograph of HRH Princess Marina of Greece.
Miss Betty Medd, Norland Principal from 1970 to 1979.
Miss Elizabeth Palmer of Fencewood, the house to which Norland Nurseries evacuated during the "phoney war".
Mrs. Mary Rae, daughter of Ruth Dickie (who was Matron of the Nurseries from 1910 to 1930).
Reed International Books, successors to William Heinemann Ltd. original publishers of "The Prophet" by Kahlil Gibran.
Mrs. Elizabeth St. Leger Moore, cousin of the Foundress Mrs. Ward, and a Director of Norland from 1965 to 1989.
Dr. David Stone, paediatrician, and a Director of Norland from 1982 to 1991.

and, of course, the present-day Principal, staff and students of the College.

NORLAND PRINCIPALS
AND CHAIRMEN

Foundress

Mrs. Emily Ward

Chairmen of the Board of Directors

1929 - 1945	Mrs. Hester Laird Wilson
1945 - 1949	Miss Elsie Bowerman
1949 - 1954	Sir Gerald Hurst, KC MD JP
1954 - 1969	Lady Baker
1969 - 1981	Mr. Douglas Clarke
1981 - 1984	Lady Atkinson
1984 - 1988	Mr. Peter Ashley-Miller
1988 - 1989	The Hon. Mrs. Lindy Price
1989	Mrs. Rosemary Alexander

Principals:

1892 - 1917	Miss Isabel Sharman
1918 - 1919	Miss Jessie Dawber
1919 - 1922	Miss Dorothy Townshend
1923 - 1932	Miss Ethel Peacey
1932 - 1935	Miss Jane Winterbotham
1935 - 1941	Miss Ruth Whitehead SRN
1941 - 1942	Miss Ethel Danvers
1942 - 1949	Miss Catherine Blakeney
1949 - 1966	Miss Joan Kirby
1966 - 1970	Miss Lucy Keymer
1971 - 1979	Miss Betty Medd SRN
1980 -	Mrs. Louise Davis M Phil SRN

And a woman who held a babe against her
    bosom said, Speak to us of Children.
And he said:
Your children are not your children.
They are the sons and daughters of Life's
    longing for itself.
They come through you but not from you,
And though they are with you yet they belong
    not to you.

You may give them your love but not your
    thoughts.
For they have their own thoughts.
You may house their bodies but not their souls,
For their souls dwell in the house of to-morrow,
    which you cannot visit, not even in your dreams.
You may strive to be like them, but seek not
    to make them like you.
For life goes not backward nor tarries with
    yesterday.
You are the bows from which your children as
    living arrows are sent forth.
The Archer sees the mark upon the path of the
    infinite, and He bends you with His might that His
    arrows may go swift and far.
Let your bending in the Archer's hand be for gladness;
For even as He loves the arrow that flies, so He
    loves also the bow that is stable.

From "The Prophet" by Kahlil Gibran, 1883-1931.

FOREWORD

In 1892 when Emily Ward founded the Norland Institute, she was determined to bring about change in the care and education of young children. Today we can confirm her far-sightedness, not just because The Norland College of 1992 enjoys an excellent reputation at the forefront of child care, but also because the principles she expressed remain relevant and vital.

Certainly there have been changes at Norland since the initial implementation of Emily Ward's ideals. However, whilst there have been enormous changes in society over the last hundred years - especially in its attitude to women and to children - relatively few changes have been necessary in the Norland philosophy of child care. The major group of employers of Norland nurses has changed fundamentally in character as has the society in which they are employed, but in contrast, the basis of child care theory and Mrs. Ward's approach to children, which was child-centred, loving and nurturing, has not altered. Indeed modern thinking has had to catch up with her approach and modern research has produced evidence that her views were right, being fundamental to the practice of good child care.

Norland nurses remain in demand, and indeed are in greater demand now than ever before, because not only are they equipped with sound child care skills but because they have chosen in particular to use those skills in the highly personal and private working environment of the family home. As years have gone by this role has become more testing and more stressful than that fulfilled by the original 'Norlanders'. In 1892 Emily Ward defined a role for the 'Trained Children's Nurse'; that role embraced all aspects of children's needs - domestic, social, emotional and physical and was separated from more menial tasks which were the domain of the household servants of the day. She cleverly described a function which fitted easily into the structure of privileged Victorian family life treading the fine line between master and servant. A Norland nurse was accountable to the mother, but was also respected by the father. She knew, like all good family retainers, what she may say and how far she could extend her role, but in her delineated nursery world, often occupying a separate living space, she ruled supreme.

The Norland nurse in 1992 has, I think, a more exacting task because this role definition has become blurred. Nowadays she is working in partnership with parents not usurping their role; she is not a surrogate or substitute mother but more of a resident professional advisor or at least she should aim to be. In Victorian England it was acceptable to delegate the care and upbringing of children to another and to deliver back to the parents a "fully grown-up" child sixteen to twenty years later. However such ideas would be unacceptable to most parents today in the latter part of the twentieth century, coupled as they are with the inevitable guilt, associated with total delegation of responsibility. John Bowlby inspired psychologists to believe in the concept of maternal deprivation, and to believe that any care of very young children delegated to another was not only inferior to that given by the parents but adversely influenced the child's development. Many people today would challenge that viewpoint, attaching greater importance to the quality of care offered rather than the genetic link of primary carer to the child. Clearly children need stability, particularly in their formative years. This stable relationship is usually built up with the parents but perhaps does not require the parents' constant attendance, and indeed may even be enhanced by a nursery nurse offering expert advice and professional support. The Norland nurse today needs to work as much with parents as she does with children, allowing them, even enabling them to share their children's care, upbringing and nurturing. Stepping deftly around the pressures and turmoil of family life, the Norland nurse should strive to create a sound and stable base upon which children can rely but not become dependent.

I believe that the art of good parenting is the gradual fostering of independence in the child, over the course of many years. The

Norland nurse must help the parent along this path, becoming a catalyst of child rearing, offering stability in a society in which family life has become fragmented and its integrity under greater pressure than ever before.

Emily Ward saw the potential of training young women to look after young children. Out of her ideas and work developed the basis of the National Nursery Examination Board training which has influenced the upbringing of children not only in private homes but also in day nurseries and family centres.

Norland's work has of course developed over the past hundred years, but it is still in no sense complete. We must be vigilant and responsive, so that we may continue to provide excellence in the training of nursery nurses and leadership in the extension of Norland ideals of child care both to the employers of future Norlanders and also to children everywhere.

Louise E.Davis,1992
College Principal

CONTENTS

LIST OF ILLUSTRATIONS

INTRODUCTION

"I wish all children were born ten years of age!"

So said Miss Jones, Head Mistress of Notting Hill High School in 1876. The remark was overheard by the youngest member of her staff, twenty-six-year-old Emily Lord whose infant class was renowned and occasionally deplored for its cheerful informality. Miss Lord approached Miss Jones with an offer that came close to the realisation of her forlorn ambition: "If I take a house for a kindergarten and preparatory school, will you send me your surplus children under ten?"

Norland Place School was founded within a fortnight of Miss Jones's assent. It prospered, and within a few years Miss Lord had expanded into teacher training. From the ranks of her trainees she frequently came across girls who had the dexterity for handiwork and an aptitude for child care, but who lacked the academic ability to undertake the formidable studies prescribed by Froebel. To Emily Lord (or Mrs. Ward, as she was then about to become) they were obvious raw material for a new profession: the college-trained nursery nurse.

The Norland Institute was founded in 1892 to train such girls, although there was scant evidence at the time that employers wanted a higher calibre of nurse than the untutored maids to whom their children were customarily entrusted. But Mrs. Ward's marketing intuition was unerring; within a few years the name Norland had become synonymous with excellence in child care. The Norland nurse was, and has been ever since, a commodity whose demand consistently exceeds supply.

Chapter One

AN EMINENT VICTORIAN IN THE MAKING

Emily Mary Jane Lord was born in 1850 in the midland town of Derby. At this time, Queen Victoria had ruled for 13 years over a population of less than 21 million, for whom life expectancy was considerably less than it is today. In the mid-Victorian era infant mortality hovered at around 170 per thousand live births, compared with 25 today. Immunisation was almost unknown and public health measures were rudimentary; many people drank from heavily contaminated water supplies, and there were frequent outbreaks of cholera and typhoid. Even the germ theory of disease had yet to be discovered.

In the wider world the British Empire was moving towards its peak of influence and prosperity. Slavery still flourished in the USA. Europe was dotted with ancient, inter-related monarchies, but Germany and Italy had yet to come into political existence. In France Louis Philippe still clung tenuously to life, but would soon be succeeded by Napoleon III and the Second Empire. The Crimean War was about to bring Britain into conflict with the Tsar.

Early in her childhood Emily's parents moved south to London. They lived in Lavender Hill, Battersea, a district which then boasted large mansions in extensive grounds. The Lords' house

Emily Lord at the age of seven years.

was set in five acres. The family doctor wanted to snip the baby Emily's tongue because she was slow to talk, but her mother refused to countenance this until she was two; by this time the doctor's intervention was not needed.

"When I was two I began talking and I have never stopped since." This was Emily Lord's own admission. On arrival at school one morning she was asked: "And will you be good today, Emily?" to which she gave the precocious reply "Well, that depends on you ..." Such were Emily Lord's recollections in later life. She also noted that, "Some of the most precious memories we have were learned by observation before we attained the age of eight." For the young Emily these included a compulsory walk from school one morning to avoid the spectacle of a public hanging outside the nearby gaol. The lifetime of Emily Lord spanned a significant period of English social history.

In her early twenties Emily Lord joined the staff of Notting HIll High School, where she was assigned to the infant class. At that time mainstream educational theory was still tainted with the medieval notion of children as defective adults, needing to be forcibly shaped into useful members of society. The alternative theories of Friedrich Froebel were gaining acceptance, however, and the young infant teacher found them appealing, particularly after spending one summer in Geneva studying under one of Froebel's most prominent disciples, Madame du Portugal.

Born in Thuringia in 1782, Froebel had an unhappy childhood. In later life he came to believe that the development of children was comparable to plant growth. He saw teachers as gardeners, required to provide a secure environment in which children would blossom with the skills and ideas which were inherent in their natures. Hence the name 'Kindergarten' was coined, and the first of these in England opened in 1851, with a timetable which has been described as the recognisable precursor of today's nursery school teaching pattern. The morning was devoted to formal class lessons, and the afternoons were spent in creative work, exercise and nature study.

Emily Lord's ambition to open her own school was undoubtedly fired by a desire to put these principles into practice. Younger children took second place in the attention of educational theorists of the time; academic fashion was preoccupied with secondary education, which had been the focus of a recent government commission. Emily Lord's Norland Place School was founded in 1876 to cater exclusively for the age group that formed her over-riding interest, and the headmistress of Notting Hill High School, Miss Jones, was apparently delighted to be relieved of infant responsibilities.

The Froebel Society of Great Britain introduced examinations and inspections of kindergartens in the mid-1870s, and in 1879 Norland Place School earned a first class commendation. Three years later Emily Lord was lecturing for the Society, and became an inspector of schools. By the turn of the century she was President of the Society. She had also been a founder member of the Kindergarten Association.

In 1887, stung by an observation that her school was failing to place a proper emphasis on handiwork, Emily Lord took her deputy principal, Ada Tisdall to Sweden for the summer to learn the art and craft of 'Slojd', a form of carpentry which was to figure prominently in the Norland Place curriculum. Many years later, in her affectionate obituary of the school's founder, Ada Tisdall recalled the trip: "I soon discovered that Miss Lord would never extend any sympathy to my weaknesses. They must be overcome or entirely concealed." This included a robust attitude to sea-sickness on what sounded like a harrowing North Sea crossing.

In the same year Norland Place School opened a senior section in response to parental demand (having first obtained the blessing of Miss Jones of Notting Hill High School, with which it would compete for pupils). By this time Emily Lord was also training teachers at the school.

The Notting Hill and Ladbroke Grove area was then a haven of prosperous, artistic gentility. Elegant, stuccoed facades gazed upon a slow-moving world, more mannered than the roaring traffic of today. The founder's reminiscence at the Norland Place School jubilee ran thus:

"In those days of long ago the Bayswater omnibus was painted green, and women rode only inside. The buses were drawn by horses who refreshed themselves in the hot weather with a bucket of oatmeal water where the cab rank stood on the Bayswater Road. There was a nice long trough outside the Mitre at the bottom of Ladbroke Grove, where naughty boys from Norland Place School used to duck the new summer hats of the good little boys. My husband remembered the time well, driving from King's Cross with his mother and a cabful of brothers and sisters to a new house in St. James's Square. He paid the tax at the toll-bar at Notting Hill Gate. Holland Park was then fields."

Late Victorian England was in a state of healthy expansion. The population was rising faster than in any comparable European country, partly because people were living longer and partly because families were tending to be larger. But growing even faster than the demographic bulge was the employment of domestic servants, whose increase was estimated at 60% between 1850 and 1870. By the turn of the century only the outright poor managed without some kind of domestic help, and the lower middle classes would sacrifice privacy in their cramped homes rather than suffer the stigma of not employing a housemaid.

Wealthier families would commonly have five or six staff, whilst the grander houses found work for 20 or 30. These large establishments developed complex power structures below stairs. The cook would often rival the nanny for precedence, since both reported directly to the mistress of the household, but nanny generally triumphed because her responsibilities could usually command more of the mistress's concern.

The 1871 census reported 103,908 children's nurses within an overall servant population of 1,303,194. Later census returns did not identify the subgroup, but total servant numbers peaked at two million in 1890, of which perhaps 200,000 were children's nurses. These were 'nursery-trained'; they began as hand-picked entrants from the ranks of housemaids, undertaking the more menial chores of child care for several years before they moved onwards or upwards to sovereignty in a nursery of their own.

As a nursery and infant teacher Emily Lord had immediate experience of the products of this system in her classroom. It led her to question the fitness of raw nursemaids to rear the offspring of the well-born. Would it not be more appropriate for such children to be nurtured and tutored from birth by a more educated class of girl who understood and to some extent shared the habits and manners of her employer? Furthermore, might not such girls be recruited from the ranks of those gentlewomen who aspired to be teachers, but lacked the academic ability to undertake the heavyweight studies prescribed?

The apparent snobbery behind this challenge might meet with little sympathy today, but a century ago the social order was rigidly stratified; social class was an important factor, particularly in questions of employment. It was discussed without embarrassment or euphemism. Emily Lord's preoccupation with such matters may seem archaic in today's more egalitarian times but it was based on a sound appreciation of prevailing social conditions. To condemn her class-consciousness from a modern standpoint would be to overlook the genuine radicalism of her vision.

In late Victorian England the notion that baby care should be assigned to an employee whose status was closer to that of governess than housemaid was revolutionary indeed. Higher wages, better working conditions and an adjustment to the social hierarchy within the household were obvious and not entirely welcome consequences for the employer. The first scheme which Emily Lord devised for the training of nursery nurses faced the twin tasks of creating a new product and educating the market into wanting it. In 1882 society was not yet ready, but the idea began to circulate. It surfaced in an 1884 novel by Rosa Carey ('Not Like Other Girls'), in which three girls discuss the notion that, being educationally unfit for the task of governess or teacher, they might be appropriately employed as children's nurses.

By the early 1890s Emily Lord was approaching middle age and was already renowned for her energy and vision in the pursuit of radical objectives. She inspired affection, respect and occasionally fear amongst those who worked with her - not always in that order. Her marriage at the age of 40 to Walter Cyril Ward seems to have astonished her staff at Norland Place, who had categorised her as an independent, strong-minded woman for whom men were a superfluous encumbrance.

There are no records of the courtship and today we can only guess at the influences which prompted Emily Lord to marry. She was an emotional woman, but not a romantic one, and it seems unlikely that Walter Ward, a retired tea merchant who had spent many years in the Far East, swept her off her feet or unbalanced her judgment. Marital status, however, commanded respect in Victorian society and spinsterhood might well have been an increasing social burden to an active woman. Furthermore, Mr. Ward was wealthy and well-connected; the future Mrs. Ward would be well placed to launch a variety of social and educational initiatives.

Such motivation would not have been to Emily Lord's discredit. Marriages of convenience were by no means unusual at that time and it is highly likely that the Wards were also bound together by enduring affection, each obtaining what was sought from the alliance. No doubt Mr. Ward wanted a comfortable home base on retirement from his itinerant working life, previously centred in Shanghai. He remained a shadowy but supportive figure in the background of his wife's public life whilst she, in turn, never failed to acknowledge his generosity and loyalty when speaking of him.

The marriage was not a financial takeover. Mrs. Ward was herself a business woman of independent means, frequently buying and selling property on her own account. The financing of her ventures was kept rigorously apart from her husband's resources, but on several occasions he put up the capital for Norland expansions; these subsidies were recorded as loans, and dutifully repaid.

No children were born of their marriage, but the Wards adopted three children from the Plumer family. The terms of this transaction are now obscure. The children called her "Wardie" and retained their family surname of Plumer, but Mrs. Ward paid for their education and clearly regarded them as her own. One child died aged three in 1900, an event recorded but not elaborated in the *Norland Quarterly* magazine of the time. The surviving two, Claude and Adelaide, were raised to adulthood and written of with great affection in many of Mrs. Ward's letters. Claude went into the Royal Navy from Osborne College, and in 1919 Adelaide was married from the Norland Institute in Pembridge Square. In 1926 Mrs. Ward (by then a widow) celebrated the arrival of her 'grandchild'.

1918 Student nurses.

Chapter Two

GROUNDWORK

On her marriage in 1891 Mrs. Ward vacated the suite she occupied at Norland Place School to move into the matrimonial home in Ladbroke Grove. (These empty rooms were soon to provide convenient accommodation for the fledgling Norland Institute.) But the hurly-burly of school was not conducive to the strategic planning that currently occupied Mrs. Ward, and to concentrate on the blue-print for her new venture, she took off to the country in a caravan. The coalman and his horse were hired to tow this vehicle with its passengers to a secluded beauty spot where grand designs could be worked out. Such expeditions had become a habit of Mrs. Ward's; they were remembered with mixed feelings by Ada Tisdall who went on one such excursion and found it mildly embarrassing to be part of such an eccentric spectacle.

On this occasion Mrs. Ward was accompanied to Sunbury by one of her protegées, Isabel Sharman, a perfect foil to the impulsive creativity of her mentor. Where Mrs. Ward envisaged idealistic ends, Miss Sharman devised practical means. When Mrs. Ward raised the emotional temperature with hot-headed inspiration, Miss Sharman was at hand with cool sponges and serene practicality. The relationship forged between them at this

9

Isabel Sharman.

time was to become the driving force of the future Norland Institute, with Mrs. Ward conceiving far-sighted plans and Miss Sharman imposing administrative control. There was, inevitably, some turbulence when the two were irreconcilable.

Isabel Sharman came from a large family in Northamptonshire. In 1883 she came to London with her parents and completed her teacher-training at Norland Place School. On leaving she worked for a while as Kindergarten Mistress at Shrewsbury High School, returning to London at Mrs. Ward's request to help launch the new Institute. Despite recurrent health problems (which probably earned scant sympathy from the vigorously healthy Mrs. Ward) she served as the new Norland Institute's Principal until her death in 1918. Known to the staff as 'Shar' and to Mrs. Ward as 'Bella', her cool simplicity may at times have made her seem more distant than the ebullient Mrs. Ward, but she was much loved for her dependability and quiet strength.

A third key member of the early staff was Mildred Hastings, another Norland Place trainee, who subsequently worked at her sister's school in Wimbledon. Like Isabel Sharman, she returned at Mrs. Ward's request to support the new venture.

Mrs. Ward knew that the long-term success of her radical initiative depended upon the consent of a few key figures in society; this, according to the convention of the day, should be sought by means of series of 'drawing room meetings' attended by the opinion-formers of the day. The first was held in May 1892 by Miss Jones of Notting Hill High School, and was attended by some 30 guests, including the legendary Miss Buss of Cheltenham Ladies' College, and several other eminent headmistresses. Mrs. Ward's own meeting of 20 June attracted 60 guests and, 10 days later, a Mrs. Stephen Mackenzie held another.

Mrs. Ward's notebook of the time records substantial support for her ideas and numerous names of those who volunteered to be 'associates'. These were ladies of society who were willing to provide accommodation for students, or to lend their skills in the teaching of such subjects as needlework and physiology. Some even offered to help needy students with fees. The notebook also lists an impressive waiting list of clients who were anxious to employ the first graduates from the new course.

Groundwork - an early intake.

However, in later years, Mrs. Ward recalled that support had been less than unanimous. Amongst some of the headmistresses (but not Miss Buss) the notion of college-trained children's nurses met with some disdain. "So, you are going to train our failures!" was one reaction to Mrs. Ward's definition of the kind of girl sought for the Norland Institute.

The drawing room meetings attracted an exceptional level of press coverage, no doubt vigorously canvassed by Mrs. Ward. During the summer and autumn of 1892, articles appeared in the *Manchester Guardian*, *The Lady's Pictorial*, *St. James's Gazette*, *The Daily Chronicle*, *Queen*, *The Lady*, and *The Sunday Times*. Most applauded the venture, although *St. James's Gazette* asked: "Why should these young women be content to remain as servants after all this priming; will they not be disposed to enter hospitals or educational establishments, or take to literature?"

During this busy summer Mrs. Ward also wrote letters to various hospitals, seeking practical support from matrons. It was her

29 Holland Park Avenue.

intention that students should complete their training with three months' service in a maternity or paediatric ward.

On September 1892 the 'Training School for Ladies as Children's Nurses' opened with five probationers (one of whom had applied a year earlier). The name 'Norland Institute' was already in circulation and quickly became the official designation. The large, front room at Norland Place School served as sitting room, lecture hall and office. Visitors were received behind a small screen and meals were taken with the schoolchildren.

During the first term two more drawing room meetings were held to consolidate the launch of the project. The following term six more probationers arrived. Some of them were older than the newly-appointed Principal. Within nine months it was clear that the venture would soon outgrow the residential suite at Norland Place, so Mrs. Ward went house-hunting.

On its departure from the school premises, the Institute enjoyed a few years' sojourn at 19 Holland Park Terrace (now 29 Holland Park Avenue), where it acquired more staff and endured minor mishaps in the form of fire and burglary. In 1900, more disastrously, the building was declared structurally unsound. Mrs. Ward once again toured properties on the market (an activity for which she was developing taste and talent). No. 10 in nearby Pembridge Square was acquired and conversions were put in hand. Alas, the dilapidations of the Holland Park house became so acute that the Institute had to be evacuated faster than planned.

Temporary refuge was obtained in a house in Ladbroke Grove, borrowed for six weeks until the owners returned from abroad; at this point the Institute moved into No. 10 Pembridge Square alongside 30 workmen. Part of the top floor was unroofed and the refectory was still a workshop. The following day the students took lunch at the nearby store of Whiteley's and supper with Mr. and Mrs. Ward in their own home. Shortly afterwards problems were eased by sending the students out to hospital to complete their three months' experience on the wards; by their return, and the new intake of January 1901, the new building work was complete.

At No. 10 Pembridge Square many Norland traditions were first established. Mrs. Ward considered that the numbering of rooms was a soulless, hotel-like practice; they were accordingly named after Victorian virtues such as Gratitude, Sincerity, Tenacity, Integrity and Patience. (The Institute's first male accountant, Mr. Douglas Clarke, when appointed in 1936 was assigned an office labelled Chastity.)

The founding trio were joined by additional staff, but Mrs. Ward presided with wholehearted enthusiasm over all aspects of lecturing and domestic work. In 1893 she wrote and printed a letter of greeting and encouragement to the 46 members of her Institute, beginning a tradition which soon became the *Norland Quarterly* magazine and continues today as *The Norlander*. She mothered the girls - her ritual goodnight kiss after prayers was an early institution, continuing until increasing numbers rendered it a practical impossibility. (Mildred Hastings, a woman of rather more reticent mien, was horrified to learn that she was expected to deputise in this capacity in Mrs. Ward's absence.) Even with her

Mrs. Ward and Miss Sharman 1893.

The Norland Institute, 10 & 11 Pembridge Square, London, W.

managerial responsibilities, Mrs. Ward also found time to trim all the uniform bonnets by hand.

In 1901 and 1902 the numbers of applications were dipping slightly, and Mrs. Ward exhorted all friends and members of the Institute to drum up some new entrants. Meanwhile, she considered alternative sources of income. The Coronation of the new King was approaching; it was holiday time and there were empty bedrooms at No. 10. Mrs. Ward accordingly offered them to employers, nurses and others coming to town to attend the festivities. Twenty-five shillings per person would cover meals and accommodation for three days.

In the event, the Coronation was postponed due to the King's illness, and the new date set clashed with term-time routines. Mrs. Ward had already collected one third of the fees due in the form of a non-returnable deposit. This windfall went towards the creation of cubicles in the bedrooms, an improvement that was no doubt appreciated by guests when, nine years later, Mrs. Ward offered a similar deal for the Coronation of King George V. This event took place as scheduled, and Norland's hospitality yielded enough profit to support the next badge ceremony and subsidise the purchase of a new kitchen range.

Chapter Three

THE SYSTEM IN ACTION

In these early years entrants were recruited by personal recommendation. "We have never advertised," wrote Mrs. Ward in 1900, "And I do not wish to begin." It was still an experimental period in the history of the Institute, but standards were not to be compromised. Those who, in training, exhibited characteristics which fell short of the high standards of conduct set by Mrs. Ward were soon invited to leave. There was a considerable wastage rate among the early intakes while Mrs. Ward perfected her selection techniques.

The preferred age for entrants was 18, but exceptions were made. Edith Sperling entered at the age of 15½ in 1893, eventually becoming Matron of Marlborough College. The upper age limit was set at 30, although a 47-year-old was accepted. (She did not complete the course.)

Evidence of good character was considered to be more important than academic qualifications. There were, nonetheless, aptitude tests for the early entrants. In 1955 Nurse Marion Read recalled her admission of 1900: "Well do I remember the General Knowledge exam, and how lucky it was that the making of marmalade should be one of the questions, as I had helped my

Mrs. Ward at the reunion in 1905.

mother just before leaving home! Telling the story of Enoch Arden in my own words was another lucky question. The whereabouts of certain London streets and well-known (but not to me) shops rather stumped me."

In defining the class of entrant sought, Mrs. Ward often used the title 'gentlewoman'. One student who attended daily from her home in Muswell Hill was accompanied to and from the Institute by her maid. Whilst this may have been an exception there was no doubt that the early Norlanders came from a fairly exclusive class, a tendency sustained by the level of fees. In 1892 these were set at £36 for the six-month course, and rose to £66 when an extended syllabus was introduced in 1903. Mrs. Ward herself acknowledged that most of her students had private means. The early application form asked for 'father's occupation', in which category the professions were represented more heavily than trade; several fathers described themselves merely as 'gentlemen', suggesting a lifestyle supported by landed wealth.

In 1901 the intakes declined, and Mrs. Ward appealed to each nurse to find a suitable new probationer to keep up the quota of 25 new entrants every three months. Competitor institutions were emerging, though none matched the scope and organisation of the Norland training programme. When the course fee topped £80 it was considered to be a deterrent to some applicants; assistance was available in the form of a grant from the Foundation Fund, set up by Nurse Maud Seppings in 1897 and funded from nurses' donations, but this was seldom able to finance more than one "foundationer" at a time.

To widen the appeal of the course Isabel Sharman drew up a system of earned study places. Ladies of slender means could apply to join as 'Maidens', putting in a year of light housework before enrolling as students for the vastly reduced fee of £12. The terms of this scheme have varied over the years but the principle still operates today.

The question of the Maidens' status was potentially tricky in a society which drew rigid lines between those who supplied and those who received service; Miss Sharman did not want to create a separate class of student who might be looked down upon by those who paid the full fee. The title of Maiden neatly evaded the problem which might have arisen had these future nurses been described as servants. A different uniform was given to them, and they slept in a cubicled dormitory on the top floor.

They were required to forfeit their Christian names for their working year, and answer to Honour, Verity, Prudence and Mercy. From a modern standpoint this might seem a bizarre and almost offensive regulation; it was, nonetheless, an adroit measure which separated their identity as working Maidens from their subsequent status as regular students. To the full-fee payers, the girl who at one time served their meals as Verity, would become more easily accepted as an equal in student nurse society when she reverted to her hitherto unused name.

Maidens were accepted at 16 or 17 years old, and this occasionally created problems. In 1909 Mrs. Ward favoured some applicants in their late 20s, noting that "the Maiden scheme was invented to help this type of poor gentlewoman ... Our last five or six Maidens were much too young and behaved like irresponsible children." Nonetheless there was such demand for these places that in 1919 a category of 'Probationary Maidens' was proposed to accommodate the queue of applicants.

In 1972 Nurse Alice Gibbs wrote in *The Norlander* recalling those days:

" *I entered as a Maiden in 1916. I had to be up by 6 a.m. and thoroughly clean a gigantic Eagle range, then cook breakfast for all the probationers and students by 7a.m.*

" *As Maidens we sat in the kitchen on hard wooden chairs for half an hour or so in the evenings and all we could see through the basement window were the feet and legs of those passing along the pavement at ground level.*"

Two contemporaries - Dinah Gifford and Alice Earl - wrote in 1975 confirming this but adding:

"*We never scrubbed floors or tables. A daily woman came in who prepared the day's vegetables, washed saucepans, cleaned the floors and the kitchen etc. Looking back, we laughed a great deal. I never remember any of us being ill and we accepted our lack of cash quite happily*".

The early training programme prescribed three months' residential training at the Institute, including successive fortnights specialising in cookery, laundry and household chores. On such subjects the students worked until noon. The afternoons, true to the Froebel tradition, were spent in lectures, kindergarten games, walks, needlework and similar occupations.

This term was followed by six weeks of educational work in the kindergarten departments of local schools including Norland Place School, which had by then undergone a management buy-out: four members of the staff acquired it from Mrs. Ward when her energies were increasingly taken up with the the progress of the new Institute, but close links were maintained for many years.

The final three months of training was spent in the children's ward of a hospital. In organisational terms this was a challenge for Mrs. Ward; matrons were understandably reluctant to compromise their own nursing training by admitting a series of migrant trainees from elsewhere. The London hospitals were particularly unco-operative at first, and probationers were sent to all corners of the country. In 1893 Nurse Ada Plowright, Norlander no. 44, travelled west to fulfil her hospital work at the Children's Cottage Hospital at Cold Ash, near Newbury; here, she earned the grading of 'very good' for punctuality, cleanliness and capability, and 'very fair' for her power of amusing children and interest in her work. Maidstone Hospital in Kent was another which welcomed the early Norlanders, as as did Salisbury. Some Norlanders journeyed north to Darlington.

This period of training was not only meant to increase the probationer's knowledge of hygiene and pathology. Mrs Ward intended that the nurse should gain *"an insight into the life and struggles of the poor; her outlook on life is enlarged and her sympathies widened by contact with people working on entirely different lines from those to which she has been accustomed.'*

Mrs. Ward clearly believed that such experience, whilst not necessarily of practical relevance when working in the nurseries of wealthy families, was essential to the all-round character-formation of her graduates. In this she typified the best of Victorian philanthropy, believing that those who had the good fortune to be well-born had a duty to learn about the sufferings of the less privileged, and to work for relief of their poverty.

After the hospital term probationers were granted a short holiday. The motivation behind this was not solely humanitarian. Mrs. Ward knew only too well that the Norland reputation would quickly suffer if nurses took hospital infections into their first employment, so a period of quarantine was therefore eminently sensible.

This first appointment was of paramount importance, being the newly-fledged probationer's introduction to the realities of nursery responsibility. Mrs. Ward developed a portfolio of sympathetic families who would extend advice and understanding to the novice. The starting salary paid would reflect the employee's inexperience. After three months' satisfactory work the probationer would be granted her certificate and become a full Norland nurse, qualifying for a higher salary. In extended form this period of probationary employment operates today along much the same lines that Mrs. Ward devised.

In 1903 the training schedule was revised. Kindergarten experience was lengthened to three months and probationers now returned to the Institute after their hospital training, for another

Lecture Hall at No. 10.

three months of lectures and practical domestic work. Written exams were introduced and the certificate was deferred until six months' satisfactory work had been completed in the probationary post.

From the earliest days every nurse had a testimonial book, in which were recorded comments on her aptitude for various aspects of training. This was a substantial document, bound in black leather with a gold-embossed front and marbled endpapers. The nurse's photograph was usually stuck inside the front cover.

The testimonial book detailed the rules defining a nurse's working conditions: she was not to be asked to eat with the servants, nor (for reasons of hygiene) to take meals in her bedroom. She should not be expected to scrub floors or carry coals. Other stipulations covered salary, holidays, laundry and the opportunities for exercise and Sunday worship.

Entries made by Mrs. Ward covered the nurse's aptitude for needlework, cooking, housework, hygiene, singing and storytelling. Marks were awarded for each of these, and for punctuality, neatness, tact and temper. Her hospital record was filled in by the supervising matron.

Following her three months' probationary post, the nurse's employer was asked to assess her social skills with children, visitors and servants as well as making observations on her punctuality, neatness and cleanliness.

Before the introduction of formal examinations this was the nurse's only evidence of qualification. Subsequent employers were requested to fill in their own comments, and books had to be forwarded regularly to the Institute for checking. Some nurses' testimonial records ran to three or more of these slim volumes.

Conflict with an employer could result in a disparaging reference which would be forever on the record; it is hardly surprising that some nurses yielded to the temptation of forgery although this was, of course, an offence which could result in instant dismissal.

In later years the leather gave way to cheaper bindings, and the testimonial books eventually became paperback booklets, before their abolition in the 1950s.

By the turn of the century the growing numbers of graduate nurses were pleading for some recognition of career achievement after certification. To meet this need Mrs. Ward introduced a badge, to be presented on completion of five years' service, three of which were in one post. Qualification for the badge involved merit as well as chronology, however; some who had completed the service, but whose standards were found wanting, were not invited to receive a badge. The honour thus conferred on those who were selected was heavily emphasised; Mrs. Ward said she expected these badges to be treated as heirlooms.

Three firms were invited to tender a design for the badge, which was to be a flower design in silver and enamel with inscriptions front and back (but costing no more than £1). Sharp-edged designs were specifically ruled out on the grounds of risk to children.

The first badge ceremony was held in Steinway Hall in June 1902. The Countess of Dudley presented the silver speedwell emblems to 41 of the 45 nurses who had earned the award. The assembled company was addressed by the novelist and philanthropist Mrs. Humphry Ward (Walter Ward's sister-in-law).

Mrs. Emily Ward was presented with a salver bought from nurses' subscriptions, and Miss Sharman received a gold version of the speedwell badge, in recognition of her devoted service.

In 1911 the bars were introduced; badge nurses who had completed 10 years in one post received a silver bar, 15 years earned a blue enamel bar and 20 years - the highest accolade, but with no recipients as early as 1911 - a green bar. These bars were later to become a source of controversy, as the tradition of a lifetime of service with one family gave way to serial appointments. Some of the nurses following this more modern career pattern felt themselves to be deprived of due recognition. Nurse Kate Viall wrote in heated tones to the magazine in 1916:

"I have great respect for the badge. I have none at all for the bars. Should a nurse be really happy in a post she is lucky to be able to stay 10 or 15 years and need not be rewarded for enjoying herself ... The bar might be a temptation to stay in a post she might better leave."

Mrs. Ward always retained a firm grip on the evolution of the Norland curriculum, making regular modifications and improvements. She was constantly on the alert for feedback from both the market and the medical profession; any criticism of the Norland nurse's competence was taken to heart, analysed and, if justified, used to improve the training programme. Outside speakers were regularly recruited to address students in training, and early issues of the *Norland Quarterly* included a section in which employers wrote to make suggestions.

The curriculum was underpinned by firm moral foundations. Mrs. Ward herself was a church-going Anglican, but the principles which infused the Norland training were not derived from any particular dogma, owing more to the general concept of Christian duty - an attitude which prevailed strongly in Victorian society. *Fortis In Arduis* and *Love Never Faileth* were chosen by Mrs. Ward as the Institute's mottoes. Self-denial was vigorously promoted; Mrs. Ward was wont to say "One act of self-control is more valuable than six acts of enforced obedience". Her most withering contempt was reserved for those who yielded to any kind of self-indulgence. Moreover she insisted upon evidence of high standards being sustained by those who left the Institute to go into employment. In 1897 the magazine carried the grim warning:

Staff in 1911 (*From left to right*) Misses Dawber, Gilbert, Mrs. Ward, Misses May, Sharman, Cole, Hastings.

"We have heard nothing of Gertrude Bell and Mildred Slack since last autumn ... If we do not hear anything before Christmas we shall be obliged to consider them dismissed from the Institute. This we must do, for we feel we cannot give any guarantee that their time has been well or usefully spent in the interval."

Provided that one could meet these exacting standards, it was Mrs. Ward's intention that the Norland Institute should be a lifelong home to its members. Within a decade of the Institute's foundation, readmission applications began to come in from lapsed members. Some of these ex-Norlanders had married, and perhaps later were widowed or abandoned; others had drifted into other professions and wished to return. Initially these prodigal daughters were welcomed back unconditionally. By 1910, however, a sterner attitude was taken:

"It is obvious that nurses who withdrew eight, 10, 12 or 15 years ago to lead lives of comparative idleness, ease, luxury and pleasure, are unsuitable for the strenuous life of a modern nursery nurse."

Henceforth, evidence would be required testifying to good character during the elapsed years, and those planning to withdraw from the Institute were advised to get a statement of re-admissibility terms.

Possibly this was not as fierce as it sounded. If Mrs. Ward had a soft spot it was undoubtedly for gentlewomen (particularly those of mature years) who had fallen on hard times, and many of her sideline initiatives were angled towards the provision of secure careers for them. During the 1920s the committee of management dealt with readmission cases at almost every meeting; some were from Norlanders of 20 or 30 years earlier. Whilst it was recognised that they would be difficult to place in employment, every effort was made to accommodate cases of genuine hardship.

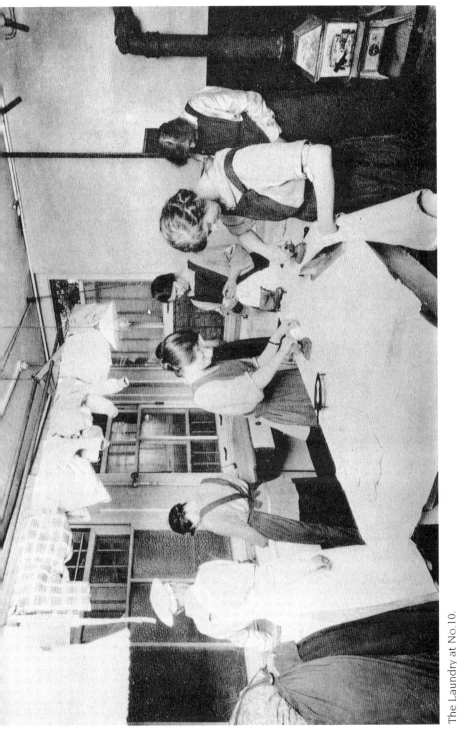

The Laundry at No.10.

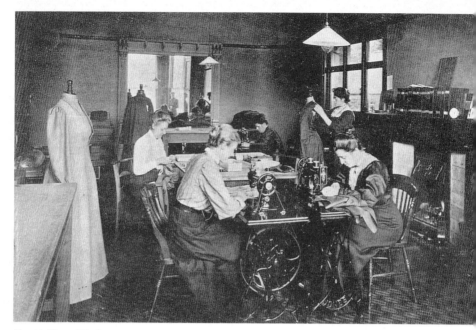

The Uniform Workrooms.

Mrs. Ward also exercised a fairly Draconian control over the conduct of Norlanders beyond their dress. She believed, quite rightly, that her nurses would only be perceived as a superior species if they adopted a demonstrably higher standard of behaviour to set them apart from lesser nannies. Indictable offences against this code included shopping whilst out with one's charges, reading while pushing a pram, gathering to gossip in groups (no more than two were to hobnob together on any park bench whilst on duty) and, of course, smoking. It was quite common for Norlanders to write into the magazine deploring the conduct of their colleagues in this matter; obviously there was a strong sense of esprit de corps in the Institute, in which rebellious behaviour found little support at any level.

There was, of course, no question of boyfriends calling at No. 10. Indeed, until they were 21, students were not allowed off the premises alone. Considering this, and the subsequent isolation which many nurses experienced when they left to take up work, it is not surprising that very few of them were lost to marriage. No formal survey was conducted until 1935, when it was shown that

arly outdoor uniform.

Students' quarters: 'Tenacity' dormitory.

only 25% of nurses ultimately married - surely a very low figure, even allowing for the shortage of eligible men after the carnage of the First World War.

There was, however, an active social life for the residents at No. 10, including regular gatherings on a Friday evening, to which Mrs. Ward would invite guest speakers. The topics tended to be either religious or instructional; the 1908 schedule included 'The Early Training of Boys and Girls in Citizenship', 'The Moon' and 'How We Got Our Bible'. The programme also included subjects of social concern such as child labour and open spaces.

Each quarter Mrs. Ward held an 'At Home' to which working nurses were encouraged to return. The first was held in August 1897, at which many old friends were reunited. Mrs. Ward's prominent position in society enabled her to obtain well-known speakers such as Ramsay MacDonald and Mrs. Winston Churchill to address the more formal gatherings.

Badge ceremonies were also grand reunions. The *Norland Quarterly* carried a lengthy account of the 1911 event written by Jessie Dawber. After a convivial dinner at the Institute, a large party (including Misses Sharman and Hastings) went to the White City and *there enjoyed the delights of the wiggle-woggle and the mountain railway which, if the truth must be told, were found to be more attractive than the instructive scenes and workshops of India and our colonies.*" The following morning was devoted to renewing old acquaintances. After lunch at the Institute the presentation and speeches took place at Steinway Hall. Madame de Montessori headed the list of speakers. Tea was taken at Mrs. Ward's house, dinner in the Institute refectory and, finally, the party went out to the theatre.

However the freedom to attend these functions was by no means available to all. Most working nurses were either too far away or unable to obtain the free time to make trips back to Pembridge Square. Life could be extremely lonely in some far-flung nursery, after the family atmosphere of the Institute. The professional status which Mrs. Ward had fought so hard to obtain must sometimes have seemed of dubious value when it set the working nurse apart from the camaraderie of the servants in her employer's household. Socialising below stairs was unthinkable, but in many houses there was no equivalent opportunity upstairs, and nurses often found themselves with only their charges for company.

For nurses in these circumstances the *Norland Quarterly* was a vital link with like minds. The spontaneity of the contributions sent in by Norlanders during those early years testifies to the important part that the journal played in sustaining their social life, albeit only on paper. Often running to 20 or 30 pages, it would typically include trenchant contributions from Mrs. Ward and Miss Sharman (one often subtly disagreeing with the other), a wide variety of institutional notices and many pages of letters and articles. Some would be nursery tips, such as:

"A little milk (unskimmed) in a well-corked bottle to be shaken to see how much butter will come will interest a child for a long time."

"Olive oil massage is a cure for dandruff."

"In order to prevent seasickness it is wise to drink undiluted lemon juice before breakfast every morning."

And from Nurse Jessie Fox in 1898:

"I have lately found a very good breakfast food which is easily made and good for children over a year, and possibly those younger. It is Shredded Wheat Biscuit ... We obtain it from Harrod's stores but doubtless any good grocer could produce it."

There were heated debates on child care, career matters (and indeed on much wider political issues such as women's rights), poems, anecdotes, pleas for advice, remedies and recipes. Various clubs were launched in the pages of the *Quarterly*. Cicely Colls initiated a Friendly Literary Society, a Botany Club thrived in the middle Edwardian years, and the Norland Guild of Christian Service was active from 1904 until the outbreak of war. During the same period Edith Sperling started a club for Norland nurses' charges.

The magazine was also an organ of pressure on defaulters. One of its key features was a list of all subscribing members, with addresses, enabling nurses to keep in contact with each other. Those whose subscriptions were in arrears would find themselves named and reprimanded in print. Similarly, anyone who had failed to pay her uniform account with the workrooms would be exposed to the disapproval of her colleagues; evidently this was a more reliable method of securing settlement than the private letter.

The *Norland Quarterly* also carried advertisements, although these were mostly private announcements of situations sought, holiday homes available and needlework services. Display advertisements were rare, although a few blossomed after the First World War, chiefly for prams and patent remedies. Boots the Chemist advertised occasionally (and offered a discount to Norlanders); Ovaltine was another faithful advertiser for many years.

Mrs. Ward herself edited the *Quarterly* until 1924 when Mildred Hastings took over; her tenure lasted until 1937. By that time a thriving network of local reunions kept Norlanders in touch and the magazine's character and function had changed.

Chapter Five

NORLAND'S. CHILDREN

From the earliest days it was obvious to Mrs. Ward that the Institute should have resident children of its own to provide practical experience for the students. She had, from time to time, taken in boarding children but the facilities at No. 10 Pembridge Square would not stretch to accommodate an established nursery.

In the summer of 1904 a nearby house became available. With loans and gifts from students and well-wishers Mrs. Ward bought it, and by Christmas No. 7 Pembridge Square had been converted into several nursery suites which were christened Spring, Dawn, Bluebell, Daisy and Speedwell. A quiet back garden led conveniently into Kensington Gardens. In 1911 No. 11 Pembridge Square came up for sale; Walter Ward bought and leased it to the Institute, enabling the Nurseries to move in next door to the main building. No. 7 was then let as a hostel to a succession of women's organisations.

The first seven children moved in to the Nurseries under the watchful eyes of two head nurses (who had received extra training at Great Ormond Street Hospital) supervising senior probationers. For the first few years Mrs. Ward herself commanded the operation.

There was a ready market for this service from civil service families posted abroad, for during the early part of the century they would not have dreamed of risking the health of their small children in the less salubrious quarters of the Empire. Until the opening of the Norland Nurseries, such parents had to make provision through relatives at home, who might well be reluctant to undertake the long-term commitment involved. There were also many more motherless children at that time due to the higher incidence of maternal mortality in childbirth; a family might well be suddenly bereft by the arrival of the third or fourth child.

Mrs. Ward offered a continuous child care service of professional standard, at least until the age of seven when the child would probably be sent to boarding school. It was, however, her avowed intention that the Nurseries should not be used as a dumping ground by feckless mothers; applicant parents were subject to stringent interview with regard to their circumstances and motives.

Today there are still some ex-Norland babies with strong memories of Pembridge Square as home during their early childhood. One who arrived under slightly unusual circumstances, and stayed rather longer then most was Mary Dickie, now Mrs. Rae. Her mother, Ruth Dickie, had been a Norlander who subsequently married. When widowed in 1910 she returned to the Institute, with her baby, in search of work. Mrs. Ward rarely rejected a ex-Norlander in trouble and both were welcomed in. In time Ruth Dickie became Matron of the Nurseries, a residential post which she held until her retirement in the 1930s. Not the least of her duties was a weekly letter to each of the far-flung parents separated from their children, recounting their progress in individual detail.

Her daughter Mary remembers this nursery life well. At No. 11 there was a large, pillared ground-floor room which formed Forget-me-not nursery for three or four older children (including Mary). Beyond that, the night nursery looked into Pembridge Square. Across the hall was Bluebell nursery, and Ruth Dickie's sitting room (containing the only telephone). A large, glazed arcade led back to the pram room and a door leading directly into Linden Gardens. Upstairs, the biggest nursery was Dawn, and two smaller

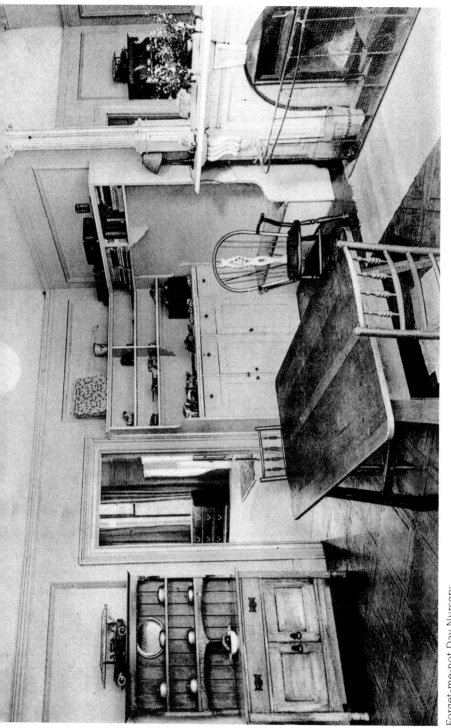

Forget-me-not Day Nursery.

Forget-me-not Night Nursery.

ones housed the babies. On the next floor there was a toddler nursery and on the top floor, Daisy nursery, Ruth Dickie's bedroom and an attic dormitory for the Maidens. Downstairs, below ground level, there were kitchen and laundry rooms and a boilerhouse.

There was a great deal of running up and down stairs; coal, for example, had to be carried up to bunkers on each floor, from which it would supply open fires in each room. Milk was slopped into cans outside the front door. Proper ice cream was a rarity in the absence of fridges, but in cold weather strawberry jam stirred into milk would be left outside to freeze. Mrs. Ward's régime laid heavy emphasis on domestic economy, and there was a great deal of haybox cookery; the breakfast porridge would be cooked by this method overnight. Despite rigorous cleaning by a team who came in daily from the Portobello Road, the kitchen nurtured an enduring population of cockroaches, as did most London houses of the time. The visit of the exterminator was a monthly routine.

One of Mary's long-term companions was John Burkinshaw, now a retired paediatrician living in Cornwall. He entered the Nurseries at fifteen months old, following the death of his mother. His father was a consulting engineer working mostly in India, and John stayed until he was nearly nine - one of Mrs. Ward's many exceptions to the seven-year-old limit ruling. During that period Mary and John were raised in the Nurseries almost as brother and sister.

They had a selection of toys such as dolls, bricks, Plasticene and Meccano, but the best games were of their own invention. A large white chest (sometimes known as 'The Pew') could be adapted for almost any fantasy scenario; often it would become a gramophone, with either John or Mary concealed inside issuing musical noises. At other times they would dress up and present themselves at the front door pretending to be stranded parents seeking accommodation for their baby; the long-suffering and probably over-worked staff would find time to humour this scenario much to the giggling delight of the children.

Mrs. Ward was tolerant of childish enthusiasms and took an easy-going view of pets, although there was some concern when John was found carrying a dead rat around in his pocket. (It was not then appreciated that he would go on to a distinguished medical career.)

Nurseries thrive on routine, such as the nightly round of Ruth Dickie to each nursery with a basket of oranges. Mrs. Ward herself would often preside over evening prayers. Every afternoon the pram convoy would assemble for the regular parade through Kensington Gardens. First, the assistant matron would carry out an inspection. Then there would be some furtive scuffling amongst the girls, none wanting to be last because the last pram to be wheeled through the gate would be charged with the responsibility of taking Patrick, Mrs. Ward's unruly mongrel. Patrick was an appalling liability; he chased the sheep that grazed in the Gardens and on the route home would stop dead beside the street-seller of balloons and windmills. The luckless nurse would have to place him in the pram and wheel him home alongside the baby - a practice not generally approved of by nursery matrons.

When the First World War broke out the prams were mobilised for a different purpose. On Mrs. Ward's instructions the students wheeled them down to Whiteley's and filled them with provisions in anticipation of shortages (which did not in fact occur).

When air raids began the alert was sounded with whistles, and the all-clear delivered on a bugle. Norland suffered no hits - the nearest being in Pembridge Crescent - but the upstairs nurseries were regularly evacuated to the kitchen basement, where milk and biscuits would be served and the piano played. This was such fun that John and Mary added a corollary to their evening prayers, asking for more raids.

Fresh air was considered to be of vital importance, whatever the weather, and probably contributed to the normally robust health of the nursery inmates. The common childhood ailments were treated according to the everyday practices of the time: warmed oil for earache, camphorated oil for coughs, syrup of figs for constipation. On rare occasions the local doctor would be summoned to tend a complaint which was beyond Ruth Dickie's encyclopaedic, commonsense medication. Dr. McLeod would arrive from Ladbroke Grove in full Edwardian fig of spats and stock, expecting a coffee and a glance at *The Times* before attending to the invalid. Minor operations, such as circumcision and the removal of tonsils, would be carried out upon the scrubbed kitchen table, with Matron in attendance. When John Burkinshaw developed appendicitis, however, this warranted dispatch to hospital. There was a general horror of the serious infections such as scarlet fever which meant prolonged banishment to the isolation hospital.

Intimate bodily matters were often cloaked in euphemism. John Burkinshaw remembers that potty training was described in terms of 'doing your duty', a phrase which caused him some bewilderment when he heard it used again in reference to the brave soldiers dying in France. On one memorable occasion Mrs. Ward endeavoured to instruct him in the facts of life (after he had made some blunt enquiries about a nurse's bosom). The consequent lecture was kind and gentle, but not very enlightening.

It is interesting and relevant that today John (now Dr.) Burkinshaw looks back on his Norland childhood as extremely happy. His day-to-day care was in the hands of the trainees who, of course, changed at regular intervals, which meant the occasional wrench; but he does not recall disliking any of them. Stability was supplied by the virtually unchanging hierarchy of staff, from the slightly remote Mrs. Ward down to the much-loved washerwoman, Mrs. King, who operated the gigantic mangle in the basement.

The routines were typical of any caring middle-class household of the time: John was taken for walks in the park, read to, allowed to keep pets, instructed in the basics of religion and supplied with plenty of materials for imaginative play. He and Mary, as long-term residents, were taken out to gym and dancing classes. There were outings to the zoo, the circus, shows, swimming lessons, tea with friends and, of course, trips to Norland's seaside home at Bognor. He and Mary also attended Norland Place School together once they had outgrown the Institute's nursery school.

Contact with his father was assiduously maintained and the arrival of the weekly letter, encrusted with the cobra crest of the Bengal Club, was a cherished ritual sympathetically enacted by Ruth Dickie. Inevitably, though, when Mr. Burkinshaw came home to England after many years' absence, John failed to recognise him from the chauffeur.

In his recent memoirs he recalled the Norland system of discipline, which never involved smacking:

"Discipline was based on the assumption that one was a gentleman and would behave like one. It was enforced by withdrawal of approval. Actions out of

Norland children in Kensington Gardens 1923.

line were described as *"bad manners"*, *"common"*, *"unkind"*, *"selfish"*, *"naughty"* or downright *"wicked"*. Each category carried an appropriate amount of disapproval which was the chief punishment. The only other punishments I can recall were *"stand in the corner"*, *"no jam for tea"* and, once or twice, threatening to send for Miss Sadler whom I feared and respected. Poor Miss Sadler never did me the slightest harm but she was certainly someone to be reckoned with. The system was reinforced by the characters and happenings in the books and stories that I read. Agrippa who dipped *"naughty"* children in the giant ink pot, Matilda who told such dreadful lies, Jim who ran away from his nurse, Mrs. Do-As-You-Would-Be-Done-By and Mrs. Be-Done-By-As-You-Did and many others were powerful character builders."

John Burkinshaw left Norland at the age of eight-and-a-half to go to boarding school. Thereafter, his holidays were spent with relatives. Mary Dickie stayed at Norland until she left school, completed an art college course and began teaching. Although they rarely see each other now there is still a strong sense of the sibling relationship founded in the security that the Norland Nurseries created around their unusual childhoods.

Chapter Six

EXPANSION AND DIVERSIFICATION

Shortly after her marriage Mrs. Ward built a small house at Bognor, a town of which she had become fond back in 1880 when she spent a convalescence there. Later, she bought some adjoining land. This was developed into a Norland holiday home call Field House, with four self-contained flats designed to Mrs. Ward's specification. One was equipped with a balcony because, at that time, sleeping out of doors was considered highly beneficial for young invalids.

The flats were used for holidays, both by Norlanders in private employment, and the Norland Nurseries. Rents varied from three guineas per week for the smallest flat out of season, to nine pounds for the largest in high summer. An extra 15 shillings covered meals and service. Bognor was a popular family resort with a safe, attractive beach, and Field House rarely lacked bookings.

In 1910 Mrs. Ward added three more flats to the development, and in 1919 she and Mr. Ward moved to Bognor to live in Sudley Lodge, a white stuccoed Regency mansion of 17 rooms. (It still stands, now incorporated into a small housing estate.) From here Mrs. Ward could enjoy close contact with the holiday groups.

Field House, Bognor.

Mr. Ward, it seems, was less gregarious with children, and preferred to remain at home playing the vast organ which had been installed in the drawing room at Sudley Lodge.

Six years later the acquisition of a corner house added three more flats. By this time Field House had accommodated the children of many rich and famous personalities, from the Greek royal family to the motor racing champion Whitney Straight. In 1938 the children of the German ambassador, Herr Ribbentrop, enjoyed a holiday here, prior to the outbreak of war.

In 'The History of Bognor Regis' it is reported that on hearing of Mrs. Ward's death in 1930 a six year-old boy in the London nurseries said sadly: "Now there will be no more Bognor and the sea". Luckily this was not so. The directors of Norland bought Field House from Mrs. Ward's estate and continued to run it throughout the 1930s. After the outbreak of war it was requisitioned for the Fleet Air Arm and eventually sold.

The Norland Institute's own nursery school opened on 1 October 1902. It was run on Montessori lines in a big room beyond the pram room in No. 10, and children were to be accepted from 10 a.m. until noon each weekday, all year round with the exception of Christmas

Norlanders and children on the beach at Bognor.

week and August. There were facilities for 20 children to be taught by a qualified and experienced teacher, assisted by four probationers.

In December it was noted that the school "rather languishes for lack of pupils". In fact it had but two: Mrs. Ward's adopted daughter Adelaide and a boy of five. Perhaps Mrs. Ward felt reluctant to compete too vigorously with her earlier foundation, the Norland Place School, which laid particular emphasis on nursery classes and served the same catchment area.

By September 1913, however, the Norland Nursery School was flourishing thanks to the success of the Nurseries. Seven of the children in residential care at Norland attended each morning, together with five children from local families.

Nursery schools catered for the educational needs of the middle classes, but Mrs. Ward was also well aware of a rather more fundamental need for day-care. She toyed with the idea of a Norland crèche, not just as a charitable venture but also as experience for students; however, she reluctantly concluded that as far as her students were concerned, experience with infants was best gained in hospitals.

In any case Pembridge Square would have been the wrong place for a crèche. Such facilities were needed in the poorer parts of London where working mothers had no option but to leave their pre-school children unattended. Babies were often left with older children of perhaps five, or simply locked alone in a room all day. Four and five-year-olds were often out on the streets.

Mrs. Ward's reluctance to involve Norland in this prompted two nurses, Jessie Smeeton and Ada Plowright, to launch the Norland Nurses' 4 Mission Fund. In the Norland magazine they appealed for £70 to fund the employment of a Norlander to run a crèche in West London, through the agency of the National Society of Day Nurseries. In 1907 Nurse Marion Rounthwaite was installed as Matron of the Princess Christian Hammersmith Day Nursery. She described her mission in the magazine:

"The mothers pay fourpence a day for each bairn, or sevenpence for two, and that includes everything - food, use of bottle, overalls etc. The nursery opens

Nursery School garden.

at 7.45 a.m. and closes at 8.15 p.m. ... The children who attend are from good homes. Most are very poor and for the most part the family occupies one room, but the mothers are thrifty and the children well-kept. Most of the mothers are employed either at laundry or housework, and almost all the fathers were out of work during the spring and summer."

Later that year Marion Rounthwaite developed typhoid and was off work for several months.

In 1908 the Norland Mission Fund support was switched to the South Acton Day Nursery in Strafford Road. The area was described as the largest laundry centre in England; 93 steam laundries, 227 hand laundries and 200-odd cottage-industry wash-houses provided work for 1500 married women and widows. Nurse Jessie Smeeton organised support for eight of the 12 cots at the crèche, where sixpence a day was charged to include a warm bath, change of clothes, food, bottles and "much love and care". The Matron was a Norlander, Maud Daviniere. The need for this kind of provision was obvious: 2,436 attendances in six months caused Nurse Daviniere to plead for a lower limit on numbers. She had only one inexperienced helper and a cook, with whom she cared for 25 babies a day.

In 1915 the South Acton nursery was considered to be approaching self-sufficiency, so support was transferred to the Bethnal Green Day Nursery. Maud Daviniere, who had resigned after four exhausting years at South Acton, was appointed Matron, later followed by Ada Plowright. Norland support of the Bethnal Green nursery continued right up until the war, when it was evacuated alongside the Norland Nurseries, and ultimately absorbed by Kent County Council. The fund, however, continued to generate income, which was allocated to Church of England homes for destitute children and a settlement in India.

Shortly before the First World War Mr. and Mrs. Ward moved out of London to Little Hallands, an oak-beamed Tudor mansion between Lewes and Seaford. From here Mrs. Ward made weekly forays to Pembridge Square in her Daimler. In 1914 she wrote:

"Although I come here (to London) almost every Tuesday I am enjoying my country home with incubators, chickens, 10 little black pigs and a pair of nanny goats. Tucked out of sight amid the Sussex Downs I play at a Canadian life."

Nonetheless Mrs. Ward kept a tight hold on the reins of Norland. Very little power was delegated despite the obvious competence of Miss Sharman as Principal, Miss Hastings as secretary and several teaching staff. All decisions regarding expenditure, discipline and administration were deferred for Mrs. Ward's arrival on Tuesdays. There was no aspect of the Institute's function too lowly for her attention, and she could be devastatingly critical. Of one cook she wrote in stinging tones: "Your castle puddings are dry and hard, your jam sauces sickly and too sweet. Vegetables are hardly cooked." This letter was copied into her private minute book, but the cook's response is not noted.

The burden of such minutiae did not, however, preclude a constant stream of new ideas. Some years earlier she had envisaged the expansion of Norland training into the production of "ladies who undertake the double task of governess and nurse". This did not materialise, but in 1910 a new course was developed for Domestic Matrons.

This was perhaps prompted by the number of older applicants for Norland training. Mrs. Ward felt that they would be more suited to household management than child care, and she devised a six-month course "designed to help women who have led active and useful lives" who would train and qualify for the status of housekeeper, either for an institution or for a grand household. Initially this training was to be conducted at Pembridge Square, optimising the overlap of interest with Norland students.

Miss Sharman envisaged not harmonious overlap, but inconvenience and conflict, particularly in the kitchen and the laundry room. She denounced the scheme as misguided philanthropy, to be pursued "over the dead bodies of the staff". Her opposition represented the general reaction of all at Pembridge Square.

Mrs. Ward was bitterly hurt. "When staff see me trying to do for these women what I have done for girls they will not raise a little finger to help or encourage me". Thereafter the venture was pursued mainly from Mrs. Ward's home at Little Hallands, where a busy social life and an establishment of several servants provided a practical training ground.

Some 32 Domestic Matrons qualified, but the market did not

Nursery School.

prove as buoyant as Mrs. Ward had hoped. Despite their maturity and experience the matrons were generally employed at lower salaries than Norland nurses. The course was abandoned in 1917 when the War drew women into alternative employment.

Shortly after the controversial introduction of the Domestic Matrons course, Mrs. Ward's letter to Norlanders in the quarterly magazine declared: "I have faithfully promised my husband, Miss Sharman and Mrs. Harold Cox (the Institute's accountant) not to inaugurate anything new, so in future I shall have nothing to write about." There was a distinct tone of pique to this remark, giving the air of a promise extracted under duress. In the following issue, true to her word, Mrs. Ward wrote nothing. However the abdication was short-lived; by September 1912 Mrs. Ward was back in the fray, writing, organising and innovating.

The Domestic Matrons affair was not the only instance of Mrs. Ward's occasional failure to trounce opposition. In 1912 she was prepared to take on the government regarding the recently-introduced National Health Insurance scheme. The letter which she wrote to Norlanders on this subject is a splendidly characteristic polemic, thinly disguised as impartial advice:

"I do not propose to advise, dictate or even assist you in this matter of National Health Insurance. Many of you are intensely 'anti' or against us women who wish to have a word in the making of the laws we are asked to obey, and you therefore will not see any injustice in blindly paying every tax imposed upon your private earnings. But I do not see why I or any other employer should be turned into an unpaid Tax Collector for, by law, women are not eligible for the post. I have requested the staff to desist from wasting any more time on the question, and to return to their proper official work, for which they are paid."

Alas, the reaction of the authorities to this heroic intransigence is not recorded. In the following issue of the magazine Mrs. Ward wrote airily: "Miss Sharman has dealt in a masterly way with our difficulties under the National Health Insurance Act." Therein, no doubt, lay a tale, but Mrs. Ward was not inclined to acknowledge any loss of face. The two letters epitomise the synergy that operated between Mrs. Ward and Miss Sharman. The vigour and determination of the one, gently modified by the practicality of the other, provided the sustaining force of Norland during its first 25 years.

Chapter Seven

NORLANDERS AT WORK

By 1914 the Norland Institute had dispatched 1400 nurses out into employment. Most went to nurse with private families but quite a few later branched out into allied careers of midwifery, health visiting or teaching. Mrs. Ward's faith in the market requirement for her graduates was fully vindicated, such that soon after the turn of the century a clutch of rival training establishments sprang up. Most of them failed to survive the economic strain of the First World War.

There were frequent attempts to pirate the good name of Norland. It quickly became clear to Mrs. Ward that it would not suffice merely to launch her product onto a free market; for both commercial and humanitarian reasons it was necessary to control the appointments system as far as possible. The Norland Registry was set up to operate both as an employment agency, and as a guiding influence upon working conditions. As early as 1898 Mrs. Ward wrote "I think I can honestly say that of our 250 nurses now at work not more than 50 would, unaided, have obtained so easily the posts they now fill or the salaries Miss Sharman has got for them."

Until 1912 the Registry not only placed probationary and certificated nurses, it also collected and passed on their salaries.

This became impractical when the National Health Insurance Act came into force, and it was realised that the Institute would become responsible for contributions.

Recommended salaries were, nonetheless, firmly laid down and those who diverged significantly from this norm were liable to incur displeasure. Comparison was made with the earnings of governesses, teachers and secretaries rather than the traditional nursemaid:

"We would remind nurses (in 1907) earning our minimum salary of £24 per year that they really earn £64 per year, being well-housed, well-fed and in good physical conditions, while many teachers, daily governesses, secretaries and other women workers of their own social standing are considered well-paid at £60 per year, non-resident, with hours of 10 until 6."

By 1917 an experienced nurse could expect £50 a year and her keep. In 1925, however, the committee of management expressed strong disapproval of Nurse Naomi Rowles who asked for, and obtained, an exceptionally high salary from the Archduke Charles of Austria, and also of a nurse who sought four guineas a week for temporary work.

The early Norland prospectuses included 'Hints and Rules to Guide Employer and Employed Nurse'. This set out the working conditions that should be sought, such as separate day and night nurseries, laundry at the employer's expense, meals not to be taken with the servants, one month's holiday a year, freedom to attend church on Sundays and the opportunity for daily exercise. At the time such demands may have seemed preposterous to many employers, but there were enough willing to comply. Despite this, life was not easy, as recalled by Nurse Nina Baker writing in 1970:

"It is difficult for the present generation to realise what difficulties we had as young nurses. This was 1918, and I had one day a month free after the child's breakfast until 10 p.m. Even during the last war when I was Matron of an Anglo-American Children's Home, time off was nil except for our yearly holiday, and then we could only go when someone could be found to replace us. I was never in bed before midnight and up again at 7 a.m. Life is much easier now."

In many cases the hardship endured by a nurse might stem from the misfortunes of her employer. In 1921 a letter from Nurse Jacoba

Watson told of six-and-a-half-years' service, during which she had been granted almost no holiday because the father had been wounded in the war and required constant attention. There were insufficient funds for relief. Clearly it did not occur to her to abandon the post for something more comfortable; Mrs. Ward's moral training was deeply ingrained.

Nonetheless, when reports were received of a nurse receiving less than her due in working conditions for no good reason, Mrs. Ward did not hesitate to don her cap and bonnet and take the employer to task in her own drawing room. She was fiercely protective of her nurses, both in the interests of elevating the profession she had created, and because she had a genuinely deep affection for all who passed through her care.

For many the ideal was considered to be a lifetime with one family, possibly raising two generations. Fifty years in one post was by no means unknown, and many nurses prided themselves on being 'in service' until failing health forced them into retirement; in practice this often meant a few very light household duties and the occasional supervision of grandchildren during the last years. In the wealthier families it was generally understood that such a lifelong commitment worked both ways; accommodation and a pension would usually be provided. In the case of Nurse Lilian Upton, born in 1879, a record 62 years' service was achieved, by which time she had outlived her charges. Nurse Dorothy Baden, a Maiden of 1917, raised three generations of the same family.

The corollary of this tendency was a faint disapproval of temporary work, an attitude which was not wholly superseded until well into the 1920s. Nurses who opted for temporary posts were suspected of being a little flighty, although it was eventually acknowledged that there was a need for experienced, adaptable nurses who could step into an emergency situation and take over.

It was (and still is) a fundamental Norland principle that Norland nurses should not be described as nannies. This word, whose origins are obscure but go back at least a century earlier, embodied the status and standards that Mrs. Ward was determined to rise above. The designation favoured by the Institute was 'nurse' but at first some Norlanders felt that this implied medical expertise to which they could not lay claim. In the first quarter of the century it seems that quite a few Norlanders opted for the title 'Miss' followed by their surname but doubtless many - particularly those in grander families - yielded to the more traditional 'Nanny' followed by the family surname.

Many of the early Norlanders found themselves socially adrift once they went out to work; as 'gentlewomen' they felt cut off from the class in which they had been raised.

"No one treats me as a lady now" lamented one Norlander in 1901. Nurse Maud Seppings elaborated on the difficulties in that year:

"It is not so much those who know we are ladies who cause this trouble as those who do not. One does not meet with the same treatment in shops, for instance, when one is in uniform as when one is out of it ... They speak in a familiar tone or an offhand way, which makes one feel that they regard one as an equal."

In 1910 Isabel Sharman highlighted "the vexed question of (children's) parties", abhorring the situation where the Norland nurse was not allowed to remain with her charge, but was dispatched to the servants' hall "in companionship with nurses not of her own class."

It is easy to mock such sensitivities from a modern, egalitarian standpoint but they caused genuine distress at the time. It is unlikely that the Norlander would have been made welcome by 'nurses not of her own class', who would quickly realise that her very existence constituted a criticism of their standards. Society was then deeply stratified, and social mobility was not the norm. It was generally believed that the First World War comprehensively destroyed this class structure, but in fact many parts of it survived almost intact until the next.

From the very beginning Norlanders were in demand for work abroad, either with English families or often with European royalty. Almost every issue of the *Quarterly* carried reports from nurses serving overseas, often in very primitive conditions. In sweltering climates they soldiered on in regulation dress, for no tropical uniform was introduced until the late 1920s.

Their experiences were enthusiastically welcomed in the pages of the *Norland Quarterly* because of the light they shed upon the eccentricities of foreign child care. As Isabel Sharman declared,

"Nowhere as in England does the child live such a separate and distinct nursery life".

Nurse Naomi Rowles reported in 1926 from the House of Hapsburg upon the unfortunate experience of Polish babies:

"They put poor mites into uninteresting vests and then into a tight padded bag ... very often it does not take its first walk abroad in the fresh air until it is six months old."

Further south, it seems, children were absorbed into the adult world rather sooner than was considered appropriate. Nurse Kate Fox wrote in 1907 from the standpoint of some ten years' experience in the Mediterranean:

"A great many foreign children of three, four and five years have exactly the same food as their parents; in fact I have stayed in an Italian family where a boy of four dressed for eight o'clock dinner every night ..."

The nurses' observations were not, however, limited to the nursery world. In 1912 Lilian Fisher sent from India an outraged account of a visit to some women in purdah:

"What a man-made country India is! Compare the life of these poor women with that of their menfolk. The latter have sports, amusements and all that they desire, while the women, whose hearts and brains are equal and often far superior to those of the men are shut up for fear that they should assert themselves!"

Frequently Norlanders were caught up in historic events or natural disasters. One had a close shave with the eruption of Vesuvius during a visit to Naples (the account of which was not allowed to eclipse news of her charge's first tooth, when reported to Pembridge Square). In 1910 Elsie Knight Palmer experienced the worst Portuguese floods for 200 years. Muriel Bois became caught up in the Greek revolution of 1916, witnessing the massacre of the Venizelists. Lilian Eadie, who entered Norland in 1894, was working for a cousin of the Tsar when revolution broke out in 1917; she escaped from Russia on the last train, leaving all her belongings behind.

Others were not so lucky. The Grand Duchess Kirill of Russia, grand-daughter of Queen Victoria paid tribute to a Norlander who died in 1920:

"During these last two years Nurse Marian Burgess has remained faithfully at her post in spite of the greatest dangers, privations and miseries which we

have had to endure. Weeks of sleepless nights - surrounded as we were by bloodshed, murder and terror - her courage never gave way. Living for nearly a year on starvation rations she managed by her untiring devotion to keep our three children in good health".

After the murder of the royal family at Ekaterinburg this family was banished to Poland, where they contracted typhoid. Marian Burgess died of influenza after nursing the children through it. One of her charges survived to become claimant to the imperial throne of the Tsar.

Other royal appointments were less traumatic. Within a year of Norland's opening the Empress Frederic of Germany engaged Nurse Kate Fox for her daughter, the Crown Princess of Greece. Nurse Fox joined the nursery of the King's palace in Athens, where her charges were later to include the young Princess Marina. She reported back to London that conditions were primitive, but that she soon had the nursery organised on traditional English lines. The Greek household was apparently aghast at the emphasis on fresh air.

Royal employment brought numerous perks, including attendance at the first modern Olympiad, held in Athens in 1896, an event faithfully relayed to the *Quarterly* by Nurse Fox.

Princess Marina learned to say her prayers in English before she knew them in Greek and, as a six-year-old, was said to aspire to a career as a Norland nurse. She made herself a uniform and organised her dolls into a Norland nursery.

The family and its nursery entourage travelled widely throughout Europe, visiting the Yildiz Palace of the Sultan in Constantinople (where Nurse Fox reported dining off gold plate) and the Russian imperial palace at St. Petersburg. (From here she wrote anguished letters to Miss Sharman about the hostility she encountered from the Greek princess's Russian mother-in-law, who sought to undermine Nurse Fox's status and poison the relationship with her employer.)

In 1910 Kate Fox brought the Greek royal children to the Norland holiday home at Bognor, and in later life Princess Marina was to relive these happy memories on the same beach with her own children. When the First World War broke out Nurse Fox had to return to England where she took up a post in the Norland

Norlanders at work; Kate Fox with Princess Marina of Greece (*Centre*) and her two sisters, Princess Olga (*left*) and Elizabeth.

Nurseries, but later she had Princess Olga's young son to stay from time to time. She was overjoyed to be reunited in 1934 when Princess Marina came to live in England on her marriage to the Duke of Kent. Kate Fox died in the late 1940s, having settled in a flat close to the home of her 'beloved Duchess'.

Another Norlander was credited with Prince Rainier's excellent command of English. Nurse Kathleen Wanstall joined the royal Monegasque household in 1921 where she raised two generations of princes and princesses. Called Nana, and beloved by all, she was created a Chevalier de l'Ordre St. Charles by Prince Rainier, and awarded a special place in Monaco Cathedral at his wedding to Grace Kelly. Nurse Wanstall died in 1967, aged 81, "surrounded by love and comfort" and a glowing tribute was forwarded to the Norland College by the Princess Antoinette de Monaco.

Royal employers, it seems, were among the fastest to realise that Mrs. Ward was turning out a genuinely superior product that clearly justified its premium. A list of Norland employers before the First World War glitters with the gems of bygone nobility: the Queen of Serbia, the Infanta Doña Beatrice of Spain, Princess Max of Baden, the Grand Duchess of Mecklenburg-Schwerin, Princess Frederick Charles, the Grand Duchess of Hesse and the Duchess of Sparta. On a slightly less exalted level Norlanders were much sought by a galaxy of celebrated families. The writer Sir Arthur Quiller Couch and the Poet Laureate Robert Bridges entrusted their offspring to Norland care. The grandchild of the Russian operatic star Chaliapin was a one-time resident of the Nurseries. Future scions of several commercial dynasties were also raised by graduates of Pembridge Square, notably in the families of Cadbury, Reckitt, Rowntree and Rothschild. In 1929 one Norlander gave her address as c/o Mrs. Wedgwood Benn. In more recent times a Norland nurse was privileged to enter the service of Dame Edna Everage who, it is said, valued her advice on some of the more arcane aspects of needlework!

Nurse Jessy Burton and two charges in mid 1890s.

Grand Duchess of Mecklenburg-Schwerin and Prince Franz.
(*Nurse Constance Sadler then Edith Brooke*)

Chapter Eight

NORLAND AT WAR

The outbreak of war in 1914 brought an influx of refugees to Britain, whose welfare became an obvious and immediate focus for the Norland Institute. The uniform workrooms switched to the production of baby clothes, and several Belgian orphans were taken into the Nurseries. Thrift stalls and other fund-raising initiatives were organised. Mrs. Ward welcomed 40 refugees into a farmhouse on the Little Hallands' estate, and was much preoccupied by their needs. Jessie Dawber, the Vice Principal, went down to help.

In London Miss Sharman was deeply anxious about the fate of Norlanders in Europe. Several were caught on holiday abroad and made adventurous escapes back to England. (One survived the sinking of the Lusitania.) There was no direct communication with those working in Germany or Austria but Miss Sharman expressed the view that German employers would not turn against their English nurses. She also believed that the children in Norland's care should not be kept ignorant of the war and, to some extent, its awful consequences. She wrote in the *Norland Quarterly*:

"We must attack this spirit of hatred and look forward to the fact that the babies in the nursery will one day be friends with present German babies."

This attitude found no favour with Mrs. Ward, who shared the jingoistic enthusiasm of the nation as a whole. "It is premature", she replied (also in the pages of the quarterly magazine) "to cry Peace! Peace!" One wonders how the disagreement expressed here translated into their everyday relationship.

Initially the demand for Norland skills in war-work was not evident and *"the conclusion arrived at by the Institute was that perhaps Norlanders as a whole could best serve the country by just keeping on steadily at their work, adapting to the altered circumstances of their employers who, in many cases, have been obliged to curtail their expenses and economise in every direction owing to the demands made on them by the War."*

Within a year that was to change; as men went to war women went to work, many for the first time. Norlanders dispersed to hospitals, canteens, social work and some even into farming. One took up work as a groom and coachman. The ideal was to fill a man's job, and release him for the front.

This inevitably affected the numbers applying to study at Norland and the Institute ran into financial difficulties. Mr. Ward stepped into the breach with several loans. The Norland Club, a social facility for nurses founded in 1913 at No. 7 Pembridge Square, was disbanded and the property given over to war workers' accommodation. Some limited club facilities transferred to No. 10 but Mrs. Ward observed:

"It will not appeal to the rich members of the club. But this does not so much matter as in the future cheapness, simplicity, cleanliness and good food will be all that the majority of women and girls will be able to find money to pay for."

In 1916 Isabel Sharman fell sick. She had never enjoyed buoyant health but this was recognised to be more serious than any of her earlier disorders. Mrs. Ward informed the Institute that "the trouble was not what the surgeons expected" and a planned operation was cancelled. It seems that many did not conclude the truth from this, namely that Miss Sharman had inoperable cancer.

It was decided that she should have a year's rest, and she was described as "intensely happy at the thought of a long summer at the home of her childhood". There she remained, in the family house of Ivy Lodge, near Wellingborough, until her death in January 1917.

The news came as a devastating blow to many Norlanders who

taxed Mrs. Ward with having kept them in ignorance of Miss Sharman's condition. Mrs. Ward replied thus: "The fact is that our dear Principal to the very last took such a deep interest in the *Quarterly* that it was impossible for us to say more than we did." Mrs. Ward attended the funeral, which took place at Ivy Lodge in deference to the delicate health of Miss Sharman's mother. The coffin was taken out through the French windows for cemetery burial.

It was decided that a Norland memorial service was impractical, given the diversity of faiths within the membership (although these were not in fact very disparate, being all of the mainstream Christian variety.) The Institute, in fact, had no formal church links. Miss Sharman was remembered at the Allen Street Chapel in Kensington where she had worshipped, and there were, of course, many tributes sent to Pembridge Square in the form of letters acknowledging her qualities. Mrs. Ward perhaps summed them up with the words: "The keynote of her life was her extraordinary simplicity and integrity - simplicity in dress and food, and abhorrence of all extravagance."

When Isabel Sharman fell ill in 1916 Mrs. Ward took up the reins of the Institute. However, she was still based at Little Hallands, and the problems of commuting obliged her to yield up some duties. To Jessie Dawber, the Vice Principal, she delegated responsibility for screening applicants and minor disciplinary matters. After Miss Sharman's death Miss Dawber was promoted to full Principal in March 1918. However, despite her 14 years' experience under Mrs. Ward, it was not an entirely happy appointment; Mrs. Ward's private minute book records conflict, expressing the view that Miss Dawber "speaks to me as if I were the enemy of my own work."

Jessie Dawber departed in the November of 1918, ostensibly to live as companion to her ageing mother in Lancashire. The following year, however, she was appointed Principal of the Princess Christian Nursery Training College in Manchester, a post which she held until retirement in 1934. Like so many Norland staff and nurses she lived to be over 90 and despite the somewhat strained circumstances of her departure, maintained a friendly interest in Norland affairs.

Wartime outdoor uniform 1918.

The office of Principal was then briefly held by Dorothy Townshend who left to get married. The staff at that time numbered 10, with two vacancies in addition to that of Principal. The number of student applicants had dropped since the start of the war - no intake had been full and on one occasion there had been only two entrants. Shortly after the loss of Miss Sharman, Mildred Hastings announced her intention to retire. As secretary almost since the foundation of Norland, she had an encyclopaedic knowledge of its operation and her departure would leave another gaping hole in the organisation.

In the aftermath of the war, prices were rising rapidly and Mrs. Ward was faced with a debt of £1,000. For reasons not detailed, she and Mr. Ward had to give up their home at Little Hallands and move to Sudley Lodge in Bognor. The post-war conditions, combined with the loss of her closest friend and colleague plunged her into uncharacteristic depression.

In the *Norland Quarterly* of November 1918 Mrs. Ward's editorial letter expressed a wavering sense of purpose. Should the Norland Institute persevere in the "coming reconstruction of life's industries"? Was it all worthwhile? The question elicited an avalanche of supportive response from Norlanders who exhorted her to stand firm and plan constructively for the future. The nurses themselves proved to have strong opinions on a number of issues, and made positive suggestions regarding the reshaping of the training programme, reduction of fees, uniform changes, increase of salaries and the need for a pension fund. Several regretted the inability of nurses to influence staff appointments (no doubt having their own views on the rightful successor to Miss Sharman) and wondered if the Institute's structure might be more democratic.

The temerity of this last comment stung Mrs. Ward into the swift recovery of her former motivation and energy. There was some experimentation with the idea of a council of nurses, but no real concession of power to the membership.

The Registry department made strenuous efforts to bring strays back into the fold: "Explanations are required from the following names who have not sent in testimonials since 1915-18 ..." By Christmas 1922 there were 808 Norlanders on the roll. New rules of

Nurses at War. (*Back row, left to right*) Emmy Jenner, Gertrude Brown, Olive Winch, Olive Villers
(*Second row, left to right*) Cissie, May Millar, Marjorie Thompson, Connie.
(*First row*) Kitty, Dora. (*Names incomplete*).

qualification granted that school and nursery work (in place of nursing with a private family) would count for probationers working towards certification. Mechanisation arrived in the Norland office in the form of a typewriter, an innovation regretted by Mrs. Ward who mourned losing the personal touch of the handwritten letter.

The training programme was extended by another three months. Mrs. Ward recognised that the War had brought about irreversible social change, and that nurses should prepare for it. She wrote:

"I am convinced that in future every home will have to do with half the number of servants that it had in pre-war days. I know employers who, being without servants, have actually carried the meals up to the nurseries themselves!"

It was inevitable that nurses would take on more of the home-making chores, and the course was accordingly adjusted to that bias.

Chapter Nine

CHANGES AT THE TOP

Mrs. Ward resumed the responsibilities of Principal although an increasing number of decisions were delegated to the new Vice Principal, Ethel Peacey, who had first arrived in 1919 as Mildred Hastings's replacement. At this time Mrs. Ward began to lean more upon the advice and influence of her friends outside the Institute. One influential force was Helen Cox (invariably referred to by her married name of Mrs. Harold Cox), a neighbour from the Little Hallands area; she was apparently a lady of formidable build and character, having the distinction of being the first woman to qualify as a chartered accountant. She had been Mrs. Ward's accountant at Norland Place School, and in 1919 took over the job for the Norland Institute as well. Another confidante was Mrs. Ingham Brooke who, in her maiden name of Beatrice Wallich had been a Norland Place teacher trainee, and eventually set up her own school in Kensington, to which Norland student nurses were dispatched for practical kindergarten experience. Hester Wilson (sometimes known as Mrs. Harold Wilson), a cousin of Mrs. Ward, also became involved with the Institute's affairs at this time.

It is interesting to note that while all those who controlled and influenced the Institute were married women, members of staff

Mrs. Ward.

were invariably 'Misses' (unless widowed); this was to be the pattern until well after the Second World War. The philosophy of the Institute included no particular endorsement of nurses who married (even those who married 'well', i.e. into the families of their employers); there was an unstated implication that ultimate personal fulfilment was to be found in achievements other than marriage.

There has, inevitably, been a tendency for Norland to present itself to the outside world as a 'monstrous regiment of women'. Certainly it thrived under the management of a particular kind of strong-minded woman who, whilst not openly challenging the male supremacy of the time, managed by and large without its assistance. This was undoubtedly feminism of a sort, although Mrs. Ward would not have sympathised with the modern feminist movement. It never, for example, occurred to her to describe herself as anything other than "Mrs. Walter Ward" after her marriage, nor did she campaign publicly on the suffragette issue (although many younger Norlanders did).

Men were, however, valued for their professional expertise, and Mrs. Ward had useful friendships with Hereward Sharman, brother of the late Isabel, who advised the Institute on legal matters, and Sir Robert Hutchison, the very eminent paediatrician, whose influence in hospitals was vital in securing training opportunities for nurses.

In the early 1920s Mrs. Ward was by any definition an elderly woman, although she still enjoyed reasonably good health. It made sense, however, to provide for the continuance of the Institute after her death. Although she had never taken any income from Norland, its assets were all in her name. In 1923 the Institute was formed into a limited company, to which Mrs. Ward made over No. 10 Pembridge Square with all assets fixed and current. A board of directors was formed comprising Mrs. Ward as chairman (Miss Peacey having now been promoted to Principal), Mrs. Helen Cox, Mrs. Hester Wilson, Dr. Hutchison, Mr. Hereward Sharman and a 'Norland product' (insofar as she had been raised by Norland nurses), the Hon. Mrs. Sylvia Fletcher-Moulton. Within a year or two Mrs. Ingham Brooke was added to the list.

The new company's articles of association were so formed as to prevent any profiteering should the Institute be wound up; in such circumstances the assets would revert to the Benevolent Fund. Mrs. Ward envisaged a self-sufficient business, but one in which no profits were extracted for personal gain. Directors were shareholders, and were obliged to relinquish their holdings on resignation.

Names were to change but the basic character of the board endured for several decades. Its members were, by and large, women of the aristocracy and haute bourgeoisie who saw their contribution as a form of voluntary service. (No fees of any significance have ever been paid to directors.) A good many have been eminent doctors' wives. Such men as were invited to join this company generally brought with them some relevant professional skill in medical, legal or financial matters.

The Board met once a quarter to decide strategic questions. The everyday running of the Institute was carried out by a committee of management chaired by Mrs. Ward, and included senior members of staff. The articles of association which defined the new company specified that Mrs. Ward "retained a controlling voice in its management so long as she felt disposed to continue it." Mrs. Ward was not yet ready to stand down.

Ethel Peacey did not, at first, attend board meetings, a practice which gave rise to some resentment; she felt that her consultations before and after meetings did not afford adequate opportunity for the representation of management matters. It seems that on more than one occasion she felt her position had been undermined by direct contact between Mrs. Ward and other members of staff. Some concessions were granted accordingly; Miss Peacey obtained more control of hiring and firing, but she did not get her foot fully into the boardroom door until after Mrs. Ward's death.

In the summer of 1942 Walter Ward died, aged 81. His quiet support of Norland, particularly in the stringent wartime period, was gratefully acknowledged but it was readily admitted that he was always a shadowy, background figure as far as the Institute was concerned. The local newspaper in Bognor mourned him as a recent but popular addition to town society. While his wife conducted her energetic business in

London he was inclined to relax in the convivial atmosphere of the Bognor Club.

Not long afterwards Mrs. Ward converted the first floor of the Institute into a self-contained flat for her personal use (it became known as 'The Cottage' and was marked by a plaque). In 1926 she was persuaded to yield the chairmanship of the board to Hester Wilson but declared "I still have enough energy to inaugurate a new institution."

The new venture was a nursery school and domestic training scheme, accommodated in Sudley Cottage. This property had once been owned by the Bowes Lyon family and had accordingly been nicknamed 'The Den'.

"Here," wrote Mrs. Ward, "I hope to rectify some of the mistakes I have made in the past and to bring up to date the ideals which form the base rock of my original work". Her appetite for continual self-improvement was genuine and laudable, but there was also no doubt a strong desire to create an enterprise over which she could exercise autocratic control, the Institute now having been yielded up to corporate management. Mildred Hastings was lured from her retirement cottage in East Grinstead to come and help with the new school.

The Den School had the capacity for 40 day pupils and 10 boarders. The Home Training Department bore the recognisable outlines of an updated Domestic Matrons' course, although it had a more flexible curriculum.

Mrs. Ward still wrote regularly in the *Norland Quarterly* with news of her activities. In August 1927 she wrote of: "My latest toy ... we have been at work for two terms." Ten children had enrolled spanning the age range four to 14. Regular parties of visitors were welcomed from Pembridge Square.

By Christmas 1927 it seems Mrs. Ward had suffered a decline in health. Her magazine letter lacked its characteristic vigour, rambling slightly with references to Queen Victoria's endurance of 18 strokes. By the following spring she had recovered somewhat and claimed to be "quite frisky" giving the credit to Sanatogen Tonic Wine. She did admit, however, to being "inclined to sleep anywhere, even in church". Like so many energetic high-achievers, she considered the common afflictions of old age to be something of a personal affront.

In August 1928 The Den was reported to be prospering under the headship of Miss Green (a recruit from Pembridge Square). Six months later Mrs. Ward was bedridden for six weeks. She was unable to write her traditional letter for the August magazine, but was said to have acquired an electric wheelchair in which, on good days, she propelled herself at death-defying speed around Bognor. In the next issue of the magazine she castigated Norlanders for not sending their sisters, cousins and friends to enrol on her Home Training course. Its numbers languished at five.

A much-quoted anecdote of this period concerning Mrs. Ward's hauteur tells of her dismissal of a servant who rounded upon her claiming "You're known all over Bognor." The reply was characteristic: "I am not known all over Bognor, but I am known all over the world."

There is no doubt that Mrs. Ward's creative energies were by no means exhausted. Advancing years and declining health did not convince her that her work was complete. The notion of "rectifying mistakes" and "updating ideals", expressed in the context of The Den School, was no idle boast. She still attended meetings of the Norland board of directors until early 1929; in the July of that year she submitted to the board a detailed proposal for the complete reorganisation of the training curriculum. The board decided to shelve this radical scheme for consideration at a later date.

In August 1929 Mrs. Ward realised a lifelong ambition when Buckingham Palace informed the Institute that Queen Mary would be pleased to pay a visit. Recognition by the British royal family had proved to be elusive, although there had been no shortage of patronage by European royalty and many of them, as close relations, conducted their recruitment through Buckingham Palace. On more than one occasion Mrs. Ward had been summoned to present a candidate for a royal nursery abroad.

The Queen's visit was scheduled for 13 August which by happy coincidence was Mrs. Ward's 79th birthday. Unfortunately it was also the holiday period, when the Nurseries had decamped to Bognor pending redecoration at Pembridge Square. On the great day, however, painters and paperhangers were bundled out of sight and two children were borrowed back for demonstration purposes.

1928 intake with Miss Peacey (*Centre*).

The Institute was bedecked with flowers. Six roadsweepers preceded the royal convoy, and plainclothes policemen scoured the area for unauthorised photographers. (The foreman of the decorators sneaked a forbidden snapshot of the departing limousine - a picture much treasured by Mrs. Ward afterwards.)

The Queen was welcomed by Ethel Peacey, who then presented Hester Wilson and Mildred Hastings. The Queen gave Mrs. Ward a birthday bouquet from Windsor Castle gardens. In return, a feeder was duly accepted for her grand-daughter, the baby Princess Elizabeth later, of course, to become Queen Elizabeth II. During the subsequent tour of the Institute every royal comment and question was faithfully recorded for publication in the next issue of the *Quarterly*. In the Nurseries, where it was explained that the aim was to create the conditions which nurses would encounter in employment, the Queen remarked that she thought most houses were unlikely to enjoy the luxuries that she had seen at Pembridge Square.

Finally, before departure, the Queen received a bouquet from Hester Wilson's daughter Elizabeth (who was later to become a long-serving Director of the Institute Mrs. 'Betty' St. Leger Moore). The visit was a resounding success for all, but in particular for Mrs. Ward who felt it to be the crowning accolade of her career.

In her euphoria she cast about for an appropriate way to commemorate the event; "nothing but the newest form of amusement" would do and she decided upon an aeroplane trip. It was agreed by all and sundry that Mrs. Ward herself should not undertake anything so foolhardy, so Ethel Peacey was dispatched into the sky from Croydon Airport. (Mrs. Ward obviously had a fascination with aircraft; Beatrice Ingham Brooke said that at one time she cherished a dream of moving Norland out to a large country estate. When asked what the Institute would do with acres of land Mrs. Ward replied "I shall have an aerodrome built. Soon the girls must learn to fly.")

The following winter her health took another downturn. There were no more trips to London, although she refused to be confined to her house. Following a stroll in the June evening sunshine she succumbed to a stroke from which she did not recover, dying at Sudley Lodge on 15 June 1930.

Amongst the many tributes which were paid to Mrs. Ward's astonishing career, perhaps the most succinct came from Hester Wilson:

"It does not seem very remarkable now to set up a nursery training college. Quite a lot of people do it more or less successfully. And the reason they do it is that there is a great demand for trained nursery nurses. But when Mrs. Ward started the Institute there was no demand. The mothers who attended the Norland Place School were, as a rule, perfectly satisfied with their nannies and nurserymaids. Mrs. Ward had first to convince them that they ought not to be, and then provide them with something better."

Nor was the Norland Institute Mrs. Ward's only memorial. The school which she founded in Norland Place in 1876 also prospered. Today it still occupies two of its original buildings and counts among its alumni such names as Monica Dickens, Dame C. Veronica Wedgwood, Sir Arthur Bliss and Sir Peter Scott. It was shortlisted for the education of the current generation of young princes, but the Holland Park Road frontage presented too many security problems.

11 Pembridge Square.

Chapter Ten

THE THIRTIES

Since the reorganisation of 1923, Norland had been financially self sufficient, owned by a small number of director-shareholders who allocated profits between dividend and reinvestment according to a formula laid down in the articles of association. Senior staff also received profit-related bonuses, a practice introduced by Mrs. Ward in the early years of the Institute (although she herself never took any profit). In 1914, for example, the bonus was set at £24, topping up salaries which ranged from the Vice Principal's £150 to the Matron's £50.

No. 10 Pembridge Square and its contents were made over to the newly formed Norland Institute Ltd. in 1923. No. 7, which continued to be let for a variety of residential purposes, was Mrs. Ward's own property, and was bought by the Institute in 1928. No. 11 (originally Mr. Ward's), The Den School and Field House were still Mrs. Ward's private property at the time of her death, when her estate was valued at £40,962. The Den was bought by its Principal Miss Green; Norland bought No. 11 and Field House.

Shortly after Mrs. Ward's death her long-serving accountant and adviser Helen Cox also died. After a brief financial interregnum the accounts were taken over in 1936 by Douglas Clarke, who was

Norland group 1932 and Miss Winterbotham (*Centre*).

introduced to Norland by the Hon. Sylvia Fletcher-Moulton. Mr. Clarke subsequently served for 44 years on the board (10 of them as chairman), and has held the lifetime presidency of Norland since his retirement in 1981.

Following Mrs. Ward's death there was a discreet shuffling of responsibilities. The board concentrated its attention on strategic matters of finance and property management, spending less time on minor disciplinary and curriculum details. Such matters were delegated downwards, and Miss Peacey acquired more autonomy in the day-to-day running of the Institute. Ethel Peacey was described by colleagues as a sensitive, intellectual character, reluctant to make speeches in public but humorous and imaginative in private conversation. Such reticence did not, however, impede her in the efficient running of the Institute during an important phase of its development: the transition from being the highly personalised creation of Mrs. Ward into a viable corporate institution.

In 1932 Ethel Peacey resigned, and was succeeded by Jane Winterbotham as Principal. This was the board's first essay in external recruitment for the top job and there were no guiding precedents to help the members in coming to a decision. They were uncertain what to look for, and fell back on the time-honoured social 'net'. Miss Winterbotham had no particular qualifications other than good breeding, a quality which was still considered more trustworthy than professionalism.

Miss Winterbotham ran Norland for only three years. She introduced some uniform changes, replacing starchy collars and cuffs with softer material and she abolished the stiff white belt. Hats were now preferred to bonnets and cloaks gave way to coats. Older nurses were urged to update their uniforms.

The magazine also changed in character; down-to-earth practicalities now predominated over abstract moralities of earlier days. There were more announcements (many concerning reunions up and down the country) and fewer long editorial items. Miss Winterbotham's letter did not sermonise on good character as Mrs. Ward had been wont to do, but she did lay heavy emphasis on the importance of good conduct and smart turnout in sustaining the reputation of the Institute. In educational matters Jane

Pram parade.

Winterbotham felt less secure, relying upon the advice of her chairman Hester Wilson.

The Institute membership subscription rose from six to ten shillings in 1921 (and stayed at this level until 1974). In the 1930s this entitled nurses to copies of the magazine, book-borrowing from the library, bed and breakfast at the Institute for half-a-crown a night for up to a fortnight per year, attendance at social events, the right to ask for help from the various funds and, of course, use of the job-finding facilities of the Registry department.

A survey conducted in 1934 by the Registrar Ruth Hewer reported that 89 nurses were looking for work, and that they could choose from 124 posts waiting to be filled. There was, it seems, no shortage of jobs in the £60 to £80 a year (all-found) bracket, but not many employers were prepared to pay three figures, even for an experienced nurse. By this time probationers tended to find their own first appointments, and the now common practice of leaving this probationary post as soon as the qualifying year was up was deplored by Hester Wilson.

Preferences were emerging clearly. London remained the nurses' favourite posting and remote rural locations were often shunned; only six of Ruth Hewer's 89 job hunters were prepared to go anywhere in England. Of the posts on offer 21 were abroad, nine of them in Paris. The *Quarterly* of Christmas 1931 listed Norland 'agents' in Canada, the Cape Colony, Egypt, Germany, Italy and New York, but these were probably for reunions and social contact rather than employment business.

Foreign employment was still potentially hazardous. Nurse Hazel Hardy was urged by her Spanish employer to flee from the trauma of the Civil War, not only for her own safety, but also to transport the family jewels away from the oncoming Communist troops. She left the country bedecked with the Señora's diamonds, and brought them to London for safe deposit.

American demand for Norlanders was now booming, and the Board sanctioned a search for a suitable agency through which to control appointments. Negotiations were opened with one Miss Bayliss but came to nothing. Nurse Margaret Wilkinson wrote back dispensing advice to those who sought work in the USA:

"A word of warning to those thinking of coming to the USA. First, do be

Nursery School indoors.

adaptable .. Second, never try thrusting British methods down American throats ... Third, if Mamma wishes you to telephone the doctor the first time the child sneezes do so; later you may be able to show Mamma that you can cure a cold as well as the doctor. Fourth, after you have saved a little money and are ready to invest be absolutely certain you are investing it in something reliable. There are too many sharks waiting to grab your money which, in the dim future, you yourself need to retire upon."

The magazine had, in the past, chided Norlanders for avoiding posts in large families and country households. Many nurses also insisted on the specific exclusion of general domestic work from their duties. Older nurses wrote into the magazine lamenting the selfishness of the young in seeking personal fulfilment; there was a general feeling, however, that the old order, as typified by the unbending rectitude of Mrs. Ward, had well and truly passed.

Ruth Hewer's survey also noted that only 25% of nurses left their careers to marry. This drew attention to the need for Norlanders to make pension arrangements for themselves. A Norland Superannuation Scheme was introduced in 1936, only to be overtaken by the more general Royal National Nurses' Pension Fund. The notion that employers should pay a proportion of the contribution was still novel, and resistance was envisaged. The scheme was promoted as an incentive for the employment of older nurses, as "an employer may not wish to undertake the liability of being the last employer, feeling that she alone must be responsible for the nurse's old age".

The new regime also signified a change in the Nurseries, which were now approved by the London County Council. Some of the narrow conventions of the previous century were being challenged and toppled: in 1928 the board agreed to accept illegitimate children and in 1932 Jewish children were admitted. This last was perhaps a reaction against the spread of fascism in Europe. Mrs. Dickie retired as Matron in 1933, and was replaced by a Sister-in-Charge, Miss N. Francis.

Nursery fees were £2 12s. 6d. to £3 13s. 6d. per week, and defaulters were becoming an increasing problem. The board was regularly informed of bills run up by errant parents and a great deal of secretarial time was diverted to debt collection. Solicitors were called in to assist in 1934. Parents living abroad and paying

Nursery School outdoors.

through London bankers were required to leave a £5 deposit.

Finance was not the only problem experienced by the Nurseries. In 1934 the board called for a report on the unusually high incidence of illness. Of 20 invalids (four of whom were nurses or Maidens) it transpired that six had succumbed to whooping cough, three to scarlet fever, three to septic injuries and one each to sore throat, glandular fever and earache. More seriously, two infants had died; a premature baby was lost at 10 days, despite being returned to hospital twice, and a three-month-old died of gastro-enteritis.

On the more positive side, there was a policy of encouraging nursing mothers to attend their infants in the Nurseries, partly because breast-feeding was always regarded by Norland as best, but also for practical reasons: the Institute had been criticised for failing to cover this subject adequately in its curriculum. The presence of nursing mothers enabled students to learn about the problems of breast-feeding, and how best to assist mothers in difficulty.

In 1935 Jane Winterbotham resigned; health reasons were proffered, but it is possible that she had never felt entirely happy in the post. She continued to be listed in the life-subscriber list of the Institute until the mid-1970s when presumably she died.

This time the board set about recruitment in a more businesslike way. The running of such colleges was now a profession in its own right, and no longer the fief of unqualified gentlewomen. The new Principal was a State Registered Nurse, Ruth Whitehead, erstwhile head of the Creagh Nursery Training School in Holland Park. The Creagh was considerably smaller than Norland but ranked as one of the top half-dozen nursery training colleges (alongside the Mothercraft Society, the Wellgarth, and the Princess Christian College in Manchester).

Ruth Whitehead was a vigorous administrator and made her mark as something of a martinet on the subject of uniform, enforcing new regulations. Like her predecessors she continued to write the feature letter of the quarterly magazine - a task which she claimed to dislike, but which she, nonetheless, accomplished with chatty fluency.

Her accession to the post of Principal came at a time when

Norland was enjoying a high public profile. The Institute regularly featured in women's magazines such as *Queen* and *Good Housekeeping*. Publicity had its downside however; a novel by Beatrice Seymour portrayed Norlanders in an unflattering light, and the board investigated the possibilities of seeking redress. Legal opinion recommended a dignified silence.

Within the profession Norland maintained a position of unchallenged supremacy among a galaxy of training colleges that included such names as the Princess Christian, the Wellgarth, the Mothercraft Society, the Chiltern, St. Christopher's, the Princess Alice, the Violet Melchett, the Dolphin and St. Thomas's Babies Hostel. Back in 1925 a pram manufacturer, alert to the commercial possibilities of such a prestigious organisation, had offered Mrs. Ward a financial inducement to supply him with the names of employers. He received a dusty refusal, and a suggestion that he should advertise in the *Norland Quarterly*. Norland had no need of dubious alliances.

The Association of Nursery Training Colleges, which still exists today, was formed in 1925 to bring the nursery colleges together in working for enhanced professional status and the welfare of nursery nurses. Its first chairman was Lady Balfour of Burleigh, and one of its early ambitions was the formation of a social club where nurses could gather and relax out of working hours. Mrs. Ward had remained slightly aloof, claiming that "the idea had bitten the dust 10 years earlier", which may have a reference to her own less-than-successful attempt to organise a social club for Norland nurses.

The Association had a somewhat chequered realtionship with Norland in its early days. Ethel Peacey and Helen Cox had been instrumental in its foundation, but by 1927 Miss Peacey had lost patience with its "unbusinesslike arrangements" and proposed withdrawal. The social club was foundering and meetings were becoming a waste of time. Discreet contact was made with Jessie Dawber at the Princess Christian College in Manchester to see if she was of like mind.

Records do not show a firm support for withdrawal, and it seems that Hester Wilson maintained contact on Norland's behalf. Subsequently, links became much stronger and Norland principals

Miss Whitehead.

and directors have in many post-war years served as the Association's chairman.

In 1929 the Institute took three first prizes at the A.N.T.C.'s annual exhibition of needlework. The categories were knitted garments, flannel garments and machine-made garments. In 1932 Norland decided not to enter the competition, as an economy measure, but further sucesses followed in the mid-1930s until 1937, when the Institute graciously withdrew from the contest, to give others a chance of winning.

In 1938 Ruth Whitehead proposed to the board that Norland's achievements to date should be commemorated in the making of a specially commissioned film. The directors consented, and voted £10 for the venture - probably a reasonable allocation for the standards of the time. However, hostilities intervened and diverted Ruth Whitehead's energies; in the following three years she conducted no fewer than three wartime evacuations of the Institute.

Chapter Eleven

WORLD WAR TWO

During the Munich crisis of 1938 it was decided that the Nurseries should be evacuated to the country to escape the bombing which was expected within days. Through personal contacts an approach was made to Miss Elizabeth Palmer, asking for sanctuary at Fencewood House, near Newbury. Her consent was granted willingly and immediately although Miss Palmer, who still lives in the house today, now admits that she had no inkling of the domestic upheaval that such an invasion would involve.

Ruth Whitehead organised the evacuation within two days. The Institute never lacked well-wishers in times of emergency, and these supporters were now mobilised with cars and vans to transport cots, bedding and all the necessary paraphernalia to the Berkshire village of Hermitage. There, some 20 babies and nurses were comfortably accommodated at a nominal rent of one shilling per week. The Norland board minutes of the time observed: "Fencewood House is so beautiful, and so wonderfully equipped, that only a real public spirit could inspire anyone to lend it for a colony of students and babies."

Inevitably, this evacuation suggested that those who remained in London were at risk. Only a few children were turning up for

Hothfield Place 1939. Miss Whitehead in dark dress.

nursery school. The directors opened negotiations for the lease of a bigger house near the neighbouring village of Chieveley, in which to house students and probationers for the duration of the anticipated war. The owners initially held out for a four-year lease, which was thought to be more than necessary, but conceded to the request for an initial six months when, according to the minute-book of the time, "impressed by Miss Whitehead and the Institute."

However, by October the emergency was over. After a month in the country the nursery staff and babies returned, having presented Miss Palmer with a garden seat which she still has. Negotiations for the Chieveley house were terminated. Meanwhile, the houses at Pembridge Square had been modified in line with A.R.P. requirements.

Within six months the threat of hostilities returned, and the board reconvened hurriedly to find a country home for Norland again. Ruth Whitehead secured an offer from Lord Hothfield to share his house at Hothfield Place, near Ashford in Kent. Children were dispatched with their nurses from Norland on 25 August, closely followed by students; on 1 September, the first day of the official evacuation, they were joined by the Bethnal Green Day Nursery.

Lord Hothfield and his family obligingly withdrew to a small corner of their Regency mansion to make space for this community of 44 children and 75 adults. A nursery school was set up in the billiard room (although the London nursery school also remained open). Ruth Hewer conducted her secretarial operations in a corner of the drawing room, with valuable heirlooms heaped in the middle. There were, apparently, some difficulties with the plumbing, no doubt due to the unprecedented demands being imposed upon it. This probably mattered little to the children, who must have relished the prospect of domestic anarchy upending their well-regulated existence. The dogs, horses, cows, pigs, and sheep which populated Lord Hothfield's farmland were doubtless more than recompense for the occasional missed bath.

Sixty-one nurses, probationers and Maidens remained in London in unsettled conditions. Nursery school attendances fell, and hospitals were unable to offer their usual training facilities because many patients had also been evacuated. Most of

Norland's property was empty, save for the ground floor of No. 7 which was let to the the Association of Maternity and Child Welfare Centres. The houses were put up for sale but, as might have been expected in such an uncertain climate, there were no takers.

Field House, the holiday home that had operated so successfully and happily for nearly 40 years, was now running at a loss. Price reductions were offered to no avail. In 1940 it closed, having been commandeered for R.A.F. occupation.

In Kent the county council eventually took over the Bethnal Green Day Nursery and removed its children to its own property at Tunbridge Wells.

The Institute thus had room to expand, and some of the embattled Londoners were shipped out to Hothfield. Within weeks, however, it was clear that the entire Institute would have to move again. After the fall of France, Kent was designated a military zone, and considered to be no safer than London.

By this time a great many institutions had evacuated from London, mostly preferring to move west, and there was very little country property of any size still available. Ruth Whitehead's mother offered to commission a search by agents in her home town of Bideford, and by this means Belvoir House was rented. The decision was taken at 4 p.m. on 23 May 1940, by which time Kent was seething with military activity and transport was almost unobtainable. Undaunted, the redoubtable Ruth Whitehead had the Institute on the road by 8 a.m. on 25 May.

Belvoir was an attractive modern house with gardens, but it had been designed for rather more leisurely occupancy. On arrival, it was noted that the accommodation was "not as great as the house agent's description" but there was little to be done other than to adapt to the straitened circumstances. Overspill accommodation was obtained in some nearby flats and houses, named York, Enderleigh and Slade. Observing the garden at Belvoir, Hester Wilson remarked: "We must make two cabbages grow where one stick of asparagus grew before".

Cooking was carried out in Belvoir's overcrowded kitchen, and there was much running about with baskets of steaming provender across to the nurseries at Enderleigh. Certain traditions were,

Belvoir House.

however, immune to modification, even in time of war; students of the time still recall the rigorous afternoon pram inspection and the unchanging ritual of evening prayers taken by the Principal. Nor was discipline allowed to slide; despite the domestic pressures Ruth Whitehead was known to bicycle around the town to ensure that Norlanders on parade were not shopping or gossiping on street corners.

The shortcomings of the accommodation exacted a toll. The Institute was hit with jaundice and influenza epidemics during the winter of 1941-42, and no-one escaped infection.

Training was split between London and Devon, with first and third term students at No.11 Pembridge Square, and the remainder of the course taking place at Bideford. Hospital training was a hand-to-mouth affair, arranged according to availability. Bristol had at first been considered a likely prospect but its heavy bombardment deterred the board from sending probationers there. Applicant numbers were reasonably healthy, but few girls were coming forward as Maidens. In their place the Institute accepted unmarried mothers with their babies into the Bideford nursery.

In late 1941 registration of women was introduced, requiring all available women to undertake war work. Exemption was granted to those with children under five and a government circular recognised the value of Norland training, promising that it might continue uninterrupted.

By this time there were few nannies in private employment; although there were as yet no regulations forbidding such work, it was considered wasteful and unnecessary for two women to care for one child. The Star of 27 August 1941 noted that "owing to a shortage of children's nurses many mothers are looking after their own infants as a spot of war service".

Norlanders turned to war work; as early as Christmas 1940 the Quarterly applauded their efforts in canteens, first-aid posts, state nurseries, children's homes and British restaurants. Later, there was no choice. The Evening News of 19 July 1944 informed its readers thus:

"You will find it exceedingly difficult to get a Norlander for your child nowadays. Mr. Bevin (the Minister for Labour) is the reason. A Norland-trained girl is not allowed now - except in special circumstances - to take a post in a private household. She must go into a war nursery".

The recruitment of women into war work boosted the day-care movement, although the initially slow progress in setting up crèches was deplored by Ruth Whitehead (who herself organised a home for babies near Bideford). Norlanders who had not already established themselves in war work were exhorted to volunteer via the Waifs and Strays Society (later renamed as the Church of England Children's Society). From 1941 onwards, day nurseries, nursery schools and residential nurseries mushroomed under state sponsorship, achieving a national level of provision that has not been matched since.

For some Norlanders the burden of war service was considerably harder. Also published in the Evening News, the post-war recollections of the Countess E. E. de Armie described conditions in a German prison camp:

"I shall never forget the work of Miss Ivy Crew, a Norland nurse who had been captured in Brussels. She worked heroically nursing the sick and the children. Even after she had been to hospital with scarlet fever she returned to take up her nursing. If anyone ever deserved a medal that young woman did - her hard work, kindness and sympathy were a tonic to us all".

Chapter Twelve

TO CHISLEHURST

In late 1941 Ruth Whitehead resigned as Principal, moving on to work for the Anglo-American Relief Fund for London Children and Mothers. No replacement could be found for a while and the Vice Principal, Ethel Danvers was persuaded to step into the breach. Within months the landlord of Belvoir, with whom Norland had not enjoyed the smoothest of relations, sold the house with vacant possession and the Institute was obliged to move.

A new home was found in Chislehurst, where Norland bought an erstwhile hotel in the Summerhill district. This was an Edwardian red-brick building called Oakleigh with 15 acres of land, adjoining a second house called Millfield.

Ethel Danvers supervised an efficient move. All that was left behind in Bideford was a minor inventory dispute with the landlord, eventually resolved by the board. Having installed the Institute in its new quarters Miss Danvers, who had been reluctant to take on the Principal's responsibilities because her interest lay in child care rather than training, resisted the pleas of the board and departed to be Supervisor of War Nurseries for the London Borough of Islington.

Her successor was Catherine Blakeney, descendant of Field

Nursery School children playing in garden. Oakleigh House in background.

Marshal Lord Blakeney of Castle Blakeney, and affectionately known within the Institute as CCB. Originally teacher-trained, she had worked in Delhi, where she gained a lifelong fascination with Indian mysticism. In everyday matters she was, however, renowned for her practicality and adaptability. Her last post had been in a London mother-and-baby centre, and she had also worked as Superintendent of Bristol University Settlement. She was a crisp administrator, a stickler for punctuality and a good committee woman. Those who came to her in trouble found her open-minded and warm-hearted.

Catherine Blakeney was responsible for settling Norland into Chislehurst. Within a year of her appointment the nursery school had a waiting list (as did the Pembridge Square nursery school). In 1943 the Institute was delighted to host a royal visit from the Duchess of Kent, previously Princess Marina of Greece, and a lifelong friend of Norland, having been raised by Nurse Kate Fox. A contemporary press report of the visit described the Nurseries:

"The nursery at Chislehurst is ideally situated. The rooms are refreshingly light with their white and cream paint and big windows overlooking the surrounding country. Brightly-painted pictures adorn the walls and there is a happy atmosphere of tranquillity and homeliness, cheerfully sustained by the young nurses".

Disruption soon followed, however, when an incendiary bomb hit Oakleigh on the night of 21 March 1944. Fortunately there were no casualties and Catherine Blakeney's calm heroism ensured that the babies were safely evacuated to Millfield. Elizabeth Harris, a student newly arrived from Pembridge Square, remembered her first day in the Nurseries spent picking slivers of glass out of the lawn in front of the kindergarten room.

In June 1944 the flying bombs arrived and it was decided to close the Institute temporarily. Students were sent out on practical work and babies returned, as far as possible, to their families. In some cases nurses took children home with them for three months until the Institute reopened.

The abundance of land at Summerhill and the exigencies of wartime food supply prompted the founding of a small Norland farm. It struggled under the management of a 'Quarterly' correspondent who named herself as 'PG'. Her early reports were

Millfield Postnatal Home.

refreshingly honest if not encouraging: "So far we have produced more rabbits than anything," she wrote. Foxes soon decimated the flock of ducks. There were two pigs called Hooper and Harper, whose slaughter was endlessly postponed by the complications of government control over such matters. Rosie the goat subsisted on a diet of airmail letters and silk handkerchiefs. "We are hoping for many improvements during the spring and summer," wrote 'PG'.

The decision to consolidate the Institute at Chislehurst was taken in 1943 but took many years to achieve. Nursery schools ran in both Chislehurst and London for several years. In the post-war demographic chaos they took on a cosmopolitan flavour; among the 50 children registered were five Russians, two Poles, one French child and one Spanish child.

At the end of the War the War Office yielded up No. 10 Pembridge Square, whereupon the board successfully fought off the R.A.F., who had designs upon the property. No. 11 was found to have dry rot. No. 7 had a tenant who seemed to be permanently in arrears with the rent. In Bognor, Field House was put up for sale when vacated by the Fleet Air Arm. Across in Chislehurst, Oakleigh was still under repair from the bomb damage of two years earlier. Two more houses, Mayfield and Winton, were bought in 1946 to accommodate the London operations, but it was not until 1949 that all the Norland staff finally said goodbye to London.

One of the first post-war decisions taken by the board was to change the name of the Institute to the Norland Nursery Training College. By this time Norland was the only training college not calling itself so. A recent visitor had asked "Is this an orphanage, or what?"

Property was cheap and in 1946 the board considered buying the Manor House at Chislehurst for conversion into a maternity convalescent home. This was intended to give the nurses valuable experience in neo-natal care, and make the College less dependent upon the fluctuating goodwill of hospitals. However it was decided that such speculation would be rash while the College had surplus unsold property (No. 10 Pembridge Square was sold the following year, but Nos. 7 and 11 were on the College books until the early 1960s). The venture was undertaken at Millfield instead, and one of

Winton, Miss Kirby's flat, Nursery School downstairs.

Mayfield.

its first babies was Elizabeth St. Leger Moore, the grand-daughter of Hester Wilson (and later a director of the College).

At the outbreak of the Second World War nursery nurse training had been the exclusive province of private colleges. Norland led a field in which dozens had proliferated since the 1920s. The older establishments of the Princess Christian, Creagh and Wellgarth had now been joined by the Violet Melchett, the Princess Alice and the Highbury colleges among others. The Association of Nursery Training Colleges (A.N.T.C.) had been set up in 1925 to promote consistency in training standards and successive Norland Principals served as its chairman. However, it was not until the formation of the National Nursery Examination Board (N.N.E.B.) by the government in 1945 that national standards of qualification were finally laid down.

N.N.E.B. courses were introduced into the new colleges of further education. The two-year syllabus was longer than the Norland course, which was at that time 18 months and was criticised for being oriented towards the "eight hour-a-day" child. There was heavy emphasis on the nursery school assistant function.

The Norland syllabus was under pressure to conform; some modifications were made (light housework was now dropped) but the N.N.E.B. model was not adopted wholesale because it was considered that each system was designed to produce a different type of nurse. Nonetheless, the Norland college was approved as an N.N.E.B. training centre. The new state-run courses threw open the profession to girls whose families could not afford private fees. Conversely, it cut off most students at private colleges from grant availability. In 1945 fees for Norland training were £165 with an additional £18 required for uniform; following expansion of the course to meet N.N.E.B. requirements, the fees were raised to £210. From the earliest days of competition Norland has never flinched at heading the league table in fees charged, believing that the superiority of the course fully justified the scale.

In 1946 120 students were in Norland training. Demobilisation caused a flood of job-seekers to enter the market and this boosted applications. The newly emerging state sector was not yet sufficiently established to cope with the demand, and the Ministry of Labour introduced an assisted places scheme for ex-servicewomen studying at A.N.T.C. colleges.

The Registry department was revived, having had little to do during the war when the Ministry of Labour controlled all nursing placements. Nurses were reminded of their obligation to use the Institute for job-finding during the first three years of their careers.

For the second time within the memory of many nurses, war had wrought irreversible change in the job market. The state nurseries which had employed so many Norlanders were wound down and handed over to local authorities, supposedly to form the basis of nursery school provision. In practice this did not happen to any great extent. Public provision for the under-fives shrank. Mothers were encouraged to return to home life, freeing jobs for the returning troops.

Such jobs as existed in private families were now changed in character. In 1941 Hester Wilson had foreseen the conditions which were to prevail in peacetime employment. She wrote in the Quarterly:

"Originally, trained nurses went to large houses with ample nurseries and large families. They were waited on by the third footman. The nursery was quite likely to be populated with older members of the family and there would be constant coming and going. Then the families, the income and the nurseries got smaller. The between-maid replaced the third footman and nursery life was less attractive to friends and relations, and in this transition stage it was sometimes very lonely. Now, when most of our nurses go to small houses or even flats, where the whole family live and eat together, it has ceased to be lonely. It may not be quite so comfortable but it conforms to our present standard of living".

There were, of course, exceptions. In far-flung pockets of rarefied society the elegant luxury of the old world was still to be found, as Nurse Anne Chermside discovered. After two pre-war private posts, she had worked in a wartime children's home at Dyrham Park, near Bristol. Through the Norland Registry she applied for a post in Egypt, and found herself nursing the infant daughter of King Farouk. Care of the young Princess Faida took Nurse Chermside from palace to sumptuous palace, mixing with the royal families of Greece and Saudi Arabia. King Farouk's divorce and remarriage restocked the royal nursery with the infant Prince Fuad but, not long afterwards, Nasser's coup called for a hasty departure aboard the Egyptian royal yacht. There followed three months' exile on the Isle of Capri in the hospitable company of Gracie Fields. Pausing briefly in Rome, the family finally settled in Switzerland where Nurse Chermside helped to run the royal household in exile. As a Norlander she found herself back in harness for the birth of Princess Faida's daughter. Then she retired, a little reluctantly, and returned to England in the early 1970s. A few years later she was delighted to be recalled into service when Prince Fuad's son was born.

In less exalted circumstances live-in nurses in Britain now earned a basic £85 a year, rising to £100 on certification. Standard holiday allowances were four weeks per year, one full afternoon off per week and, of course, the opportunity to worship on Sundays.

Chapter Thirteen

POST WAR: A NEW WORLD OF NURSERY NURSING

Catherine Blakeney retired in the spring of 1949. Like most of Norland's ex-Principals she kept in touch right up to her death in 1977 at the age of 91. Her successor was Joan Kirby, a social science graduate of the London School of Economics and an experienced almoner. Following three jobs with London hospitals Miss Kirby worked as a welfare officer with the government of Jamaica, and served during the war as an A.T.S. staff captain. Contemporaries recalled her "pleasing appearance, tall and dark with a frank manner; an excellent speaker, fluent and to the point".

She came to Norland with a fistful of glowing references to undertake a difficult task. The College was now experiencing the full brunt of post-war austerity. Social changes had reshaped the employment market for nurses, and a new state sector obliged Norland to sustain its pre-eminence without compromise of standards.

Furthermore, a spate of legislation affected many aspects of Norland's operation. Public health and children were major political preoccupations, resulting in new statutes setting up the N.H.S., co-ordinating the registration of births and deaths, and regulating the administration of child welfare. The introduction of

Miss Kirby (*Centre left*) with staff.

penicillin and polio vaccine were important steps forward in child health. Mass antenatal care was organised for the first time.

In addition to the burden of implementing change at Norland, Joan Kirby sought and obtained committee membership of the N.N.E.B. and A.N.T.C., from which she was in a commanding position to influence decisions that were to shape the future of the nursing profession.

Hester Wilson died in 1949. Three years previously she had retired from the chairmanship of the Norland board, thus (temporarily) severing the dynastic link between the board and the College's founder, Mrs. Ward. Since easing her elderly cousin somewhat reluctantly into retirement in the late 1920s, Mrs. Wilson had ensured a consistency of purpose throughout the tenure of four Principals, each of whom gratefully acknowledged her profoundly commonsense attitude to the implementation of Norland ideals. In the early days of her membership the board had been deeply involved with the minutiae of the Institute's operation - perhaps not a cost-effective use of directors' time by modern standards, but it did impart a thorough awareness of the basic human mechanics which underpinned the Institute's success.

In the post-war years the board was, inevitably, much more engrossed with financial survival and property management. However the chairman Sir Gerald Hurst, doctor and magistrate, still found time to share his expert knowledge of adoption procedures with Norland students, who were often admitted to the gallery of his court in Bromley to learn from its proceedings. Another member was Mrs. Baker, wife of an Air Vice-Marshal, and later to become Lady Baker. She too had a reputation for 'hands-on' directorship. Meetings may well have been attended in grand hats, but she was equally at home with sleeves rolled up, clearing out a Norland cupboard. Lady Baker became chairman of the board in 1955, a post which she held for 14 years.

Joan Kirby's reforms included the abolition of nurses' testimonial books and a curriculum change that introduced a four-and-a-half-month stint of nursery school experience. Despite initial opposition to some of the detail in the N.N.E.B. syllabus it became necessary to make some amendments to keep Norland within the parameters of approval. Joan Kirby also had to accommodate the demands of new legislation, which brought the College into close contact with the Ministries of Health and Education.

She also brought about the final demise of the bar system which rewarded nurses for a lifetime's employment in the service of one family. Such appointments were now unknown, except in the very grandest of households. Attempts to undercut Norland's endorsement of this practice had been made by a succession of nurses since 1900, but their radical opinions had been outweighed by the general consensus. In 1958 the pro-bar lobby was no longer large enough to prevail and Joan Kirby's view was expressed thus:

"In these days of small families, many with limited means, even the very best nurse will be regarded as a luxury after the children are well-established and nearing school age".

Permanence was no longer the pinnacle of career achievement. However, bar nurses continued to be listed in the annual members' index, published in the magazine; in 1961 there were 21 green bar-holders (denoting 21 years' service), seven blues (15 years) and 24 silver bars (10 years).

The following year Joan Kirby introduced the speedwell badge, a Norland emblem for nurses who no longer wore the Norland uniform at work. It was available to any certificated nurse on payment of fourteen shillings and ninepence. In the *Norland Quarterly* she wrote:

"The need for this badge has been felt for a very long time, particularly by those of you who are working in hospitals, nurseries or other institutions where uniform other than Norland's is provided. It in no way takes the place of the old badge awarded for long service in one post".

Thus it was implied that the three-year post with one family, necessary to qualify for the old badge, was no longer the norm. However there was to be no relaxation in the standards of conduct and dress expected from Norlanders. The *Norland Quarterly* of December 1956 contained a sharp reprimand from the Principal who had spotted a nurse pushing a pram on which was displayed a political poster; with or without the employer's permission this was considered unacceptable behaviour. The same issue carried letters from two older nurses reporting and deploring sightings of sandals and ear-rings on Norlanders.

In 1956 the now familiar tradition of the annual Norland Garden Party was inaugurated, replacing the old-style open days. The star guests during these years were often first-generation Norlanders, now approaching their eighties and still actively interested in College developments. Nurses Dorothy Cross, Nina Baker and Kate Fraser were among the pre-World War One graduates who attended, together with Mildred Hastings who had retired as secretary just after the First World War, but kept up a regular correspondence with the College. Ex-Principals Dawber, Peacey, Winterbotham and Blakeney were among the hundreds of life subscribers now on the College membership list.

The magazine, which in wartime had been reduced to an annual letter from the Principal, was restored to twice-yearly publication, though it retained its name as the *Norland Quarterly*. It was now octavo rather than quarto but each issue still led with the Principal's letter. Joan Kirby's style was newsy and chatty, far removed from the rather distant, didactic tone of pre-war Principals. Contributions from Norlanders included a high proportion of accounts describing service abroad, perhaps because these nurses felt a more acute need to keep in touch.

Despite the strained economic conditions a small profit was

made in 1954. A school bus was bought and the College acquired another property next door to Mayfield. It was hoped that this house, called Winton, might eventually be linked up with its neighbour. The College was now scattered amongst four properties, one of which was sited across a main road. Mary Ann Gibbs, author of "The Years of the Nannies", visited in the late 1950s and described her approach to the College thus:

"I got out of the train at Chislehurst and made my way up the hill in surroundings that still bore traces of the country district that it was, not so very long ago. When I got to the archway that spanned the road at the top I turned and faced into a bracing wind that met me across the common. The houses that form the College have extensive gardens and a horticulturist produces most of the fruit and vegetables for the College".

The separation of College operations into four sites, each requiring a resident housemistress, was obviously inefficient and inconvenient. During the exceptionally hard winter of 1961/62 nurses and staff had to use the outside footpath because the garden staff were unable to keep the others open. The hardship was keenly felt. Plans for joining Winton and Mayfield were discarded in favour of a major project whereby some land would be sold for development, financing a single, purpose-built home of the entire College.

In 1963 a New Building Fund was launched and sustained by a programme of social events for the nurses. An Autumn Fair was held at Winton and, with the vigorous participation of Lady Baker, raised nearly £500. In the same year the first Norland dance was held in the College grounds. It is interesting to note that it was the need to raise funds that initially eased some of the traditionally Draconian restrictions on nurses' social lives.

Finance was not the only hurdle, however. The project was beset with planning hitches arising from the College's location on the edge of Chislehurst Common. Nonetheless, in December 1964 planning consent was received for a brand new college on the Mayfield site. In May 1965 it was believed that a start to building was imminent. The Nurseries moved into Oakleigh in anticipation of the upheaval. Fruit trees were transplanted from around Winton. A building called Elm House was rented for probationer accommodation.

However the financial climate turned cold once again; the credit squeeze of mid-1964 scotched mortgage prospects and the project was deferred indefinitely. Joan Kirby, now approaching retirement age and suffering from heart trouble, resigned, expressing the hope that she might be succeeded by a Norlander. In her last letter to the magazine she encouraged members to apply for her post. She retired to live with her brother in Horsham and, from there, served as chairman of the various Norland charity funds.

Her replacement, introduced by Lady Baker, was Lucy Keymer who took office in April 1966. Lucy Keymer was educated at St. Swithin's in Winchester, after which she held several administrative and managerial appointments including a close involvement with the project to rebuild Coventry Cathedral. More recently she had been personnel officer to a firm of London solicitors. Much of her work had an ecclesiastical bias, reflecting a deep commitment to the Anglican church.

Thus she was well versed in the administrative and financial processes surrounding construction projects, but she lacked any specific experience with children or education. Given the vicissitudes of the Chislehurst plans, it was understandable that the board should have favoured the appointment of someone who would grasp the negotiations, and resolve the long-standing problem of the College's accommodation.

Within months of Lucy Keymer's arrival it was decided that the uncertainties and shortcomings of adapting the Chislehurst property called for a change of policy. The building fund contained £700, and some cash had been released by the final disposal of No. 10 Pembridge Square (the sale having completed in 1965). The long-awaited building licence eventually came through but by now the developers Wates were interested in buying all the Chislehurst land, and it was decided to look for one, large house elsewhere. Lucy Keymer and Lady Baker conducted a tour of country houses on the market, beginning with Denford Park in West Berkshire. In subsequent visits to other houses they found nothing to match its potential facilities, and an offer was duly made.

Chapter Fourteen

LEAN YEARS

Six miles west of Newbury, Denford is a tiny hamlet dominated by the Georgian mansion of Denford Park. A manor of sorts, known as 'Daneford' existed here from Saxon times, within the bounds of what was then the market town of Kintbury on the river Kennet. Records indicate its subsequent transfer into Norman hands, and in the thirteenth century Edward I was entertained at a house here.

Later, the Denford estate passed to the Duchy of Lancaster, and thence through the hands of several families. The present house was built in 1832, or perhaps a little earlier, to the design of Sir Jeffry Wyatville. Nikolaus Pevsner, in chronicling the county's architectural heritage, describes it as "a stone house of three bays, spaciously planned". At around the same time, a Chapel of the Holy Trinity was built in the grounds. Today it is more closely associated with the town of Hungerford, which has long since outgrown its neighbouring village of Kintbury.

Denford Park remained a private residence until the Second World War. In 1939 the owners bequeathed it to the Order of the Holy Sepulchre, a community of Roman Catholic nuns originally founded in Liege. Their full occupancy of the house was, however, presumably deferred because Denford was soon to be

Denford Park, Hungerford, Berkshire.

requisitioned for the billeting of American forces.

In the mid-1950s the convent established a preparatory school for girls in the house and its 150 acres of grounds. (Shortly after this time the Victorian Gothic chapel in the grounds was demolished). In 1967, with dwindling numbers of pupils, the junior school was to be amalgamated with its senior sibling in Chelmsford.

There were many uncertainties regarding the viability of Norland in such a remote location. Supporters of the move pointed to the centrality of the position, which could benefit from good links with the Midlands and the West as well as London (although at that time the M4 Motorway ended at Reading). Pessimists wondered where the children would come from to fill the nursery school, and how keen would young girls be to embark on a course situated in such rural isolation.

These doubts notwithstanding, the board approved the move. Lady Baker immersed herself in detailed planning, even to the extent of making scale cut-outs of beds and cots to fit into the Denford accommodation layout. Both she and Lucy Keymer made numerous trips to assess the facilities in advance of the move.

For Douglas Clarke, as financial adviser to the board, it was a bold and far-sighted decision: a gamble, some might even have said. Certainly its returns were not immediate, and the next few years were a testing time for the College.

The Chislehurst sites were sold for a considerable sum to the building firm Wates, but the purchase of Denford and subsequent essential modifications absorbed these funds. The Building Fund, for which the students had worked so hard, stood at around £700 and this was allocated to improving accommodation. However, the College was operating at a loss even before the departure from Chislehurst. A bank loan was necessary to keep business afloat, and the servicing of this debt was to weigh heavily upon College finances for several years.

The move took place in the late summer of 1967, within days of the nuns' departure. During two weeks some 20 van-loads transferred the College from Chislehurst to Denford. Shortly after Norland's arrival two visitors arrived to wish the nuns God speed, only to find that they were too late, but by happy coincidence one of them proved to be a Norlander. In the warmth of the August sunshine the students set to in swimsuits to scrub and commission the outdoor swimming pool - a luxury previously undreamed of!

Under the single roof of Denford Park there was ample space for probationers, nurses, babies and staff. Rolling parkland surrounded the elegant mansion; most of it was leased to a nearby farmer, whose sheep and deer could be seen grazing peacefully under magnificent oak, beech and cedar trees. A walled garden offered peaceful seclusion for pensive walkers.

The accommodation was extensive, but not ideally appointed. Some elegant rooms remained as testimony to the grand lifestyle of bygone inhabitants but the convent regime prescribed spartan living conditions. By comparison with mainstream further education establishments, Norland students' accommodation was primitive. Students slept in what were still, essentially, the prep school dormitories, seven or eight to a room with minimal heating and no carpets. Those who moved from Chislehurst may have overlooked these conditions in their delight at being all under one roof, but subsequent intakes, with no experience of inferior conditions, looked askance at the facilities.

Student numbers began to fall, but they received an artificial boost shortly after the move to Denford with the demise of the Violet Melchett Training College; some eight or nine N.N.E.B. students who had not completed their courses transferred to Norland. However, there was little to celebrate in the collapse of a competitor. The economic and social climate could well find more victims from among the reduced numbers of private colleges.

Mindful of the drop in entry applications, the board agreed to waive the third 'O' level requirement and reduce the age minimum from 18 to 17½ (to boost the traditionally low May intake). There was a concerted effort to recruit from state schools as well as from the private sector.

It was agreed by the directors that to increase its student appeal the College should be run more along the lines of a university, and less like a school. Rules of conduct should be less oppressive and more social activities would be promoted. It was even conceded that students might entertain parents and boyfriends in College.

Students were welcome to bring their own cars, although only about 10 ran to the extravagance; there were, by comparison, some 30 or 40 bikes in the sheds. Transport of some sort was vital; the small town of Hungerford was a stiff walk away, and Newbury, with its cinema, sports facilities and chain store shopping a full nine miles. The College soon had to invest some of its scant resources in a minibus to fetch and carry students and nursery school pupils.

Several key staff had, inevitably, been lost in the move. Two teachers from the nursery school, the domestic science teacher, the book-keeper, caterer and gardener were among those for whom replacements had to be found at Denford.

Within two years Mrs. Guyler, the long serving and stalwart Matron of the Nurseries handed in her resignation. It was acknowledged by Lucy Keymer that the lack of adequate staff in the Nurseries had contributed to her ill-health and departure. There followed eleven months with no Matron.

Another major loss consequent upon the move was the resignation of Lady Baker from chairmanship of the board. The strain of travel from her home in Chislehurst, where she had previously been a neighbour to the College, dictated a retreat. She had, in any case, many other deserving commitments, among them a dedication to the Red Cross.

The Nurseries experienced a predictable fall-off in numbers when transported to the Berkshire countryside but within a year had recovered to maximum capacity of 24. However this level was not subsequently sustained. There were times when there were too few babies in residence for nurses to gain their prescribed experience, and Lucy Keymer was obliged to farm students out to hospitals for an extra term. Initially there were problems establishing the necessary hospital facilities; the long relationship with Farnborough Hospital was severed on account of distance, only to be reinstated when an alternative arrangement with the Radcliffe Infirmary in Oxford failed to work out.

The nursery school left a roll of 35 children behind in Chislehurst. Although some 30 enquiries were fielded in advance of the Denford move, directors were sufficiently worried about the problems of access to cut fees from 35 guineas to 25 guineas per term. The new term opened with just six children, and the road

Miss Keymer.

back to full occupancy was to prove long and hard, given the scattered population of the catchment area and the recent growth of the playgroup movement. To widen its appeal the school created a new 'pre-preparatory' or 'pre-reception' class intended to separate the rising-five year olds and prepare them for starting school.

The board was deeply preoccupied with the worsening financial position. In the late sixties the bank pressured heavily for a reduction in the College debt, such that various investments had to be sold, and at one time a mortgage on the Denford property was even considered; this proved to be unobtainable at the time when it was wanted.

Economy was the order of the day. The *Norland Quarterly*, which had not been published quarterly since before the war, was cut back from two issues a year to one, and given the more realistic title of *The Norlander*. In 1968 the directors agreed to waive their fees and expenses for an indefinite period; these emoluments were not restored until 1976.

One of Miss Keymer's strengths was a natural sense of style, which translated into the outward appearance presented by the College. She modified the uniform, introducing the elegant bowlers (still worn by nurses today) to replace the slightly frumpish pre-war hats. The brown nylon mac was replaced by a poplin raincoat of more modern cut. Funds for interior decoration were strictly limited, so Miss Keymer negotiated with the Berkshire Art Gallery Schools Service for the loan of pictures from a circulating stock.

In the wider world Norland made its presence felt at high profile events such as the Badminton Three Day Event, at which Miss Keymer organised the first Norland crèche. Parties of foreign visitors converged on Denford to study the renowned formula. Despite its serious financial problems Norland maintained its pre-eminence in the general public perception, an achievement to the credit of Miss Keymer's presentational skills.

However, within the profession, the Principal's inexperience in the field of education was beginning to tell. The curriculum languished, and became a target for criticism by the N.N.E.B., which, although granting examination status to the College, maintained pressure against what was considered to be Norland's adherence to a 'finishing school' approach to nursery nurse training. The lecture timetable was considered inadequate; students still spent an excessive proportion of syllabus time on tasks such as laundry and catering. Such were the lack of resources it became necessary to transport students to Reading Technical College for tuition in health studies. In the autumn of 1970 the Director of Studies resigned, leading to complaints from parents about the shortage of lectures. It became clear that a radical change in management was needed.

Chapter Fifteen

THE SEVENTIES

In the autumn of 1970 Lucy Keymer announced her resignation, ending five year's service which spanned one of Norland's most difficult periods. In *The Norlander* she wrote: "*There is general agreement among the directors that the time has come for a wide reorganisation of the educational side of Norland training to bring it more into line with modern teaching methods. Such reorganisation calls for someone younger than myself, and with specific qualifications*."

Miss Keymer moved to Alresford to enjoy an active retirement working for the Anglican church, and on the roll of honorary life subscribers she joined her surviving predecessors Misses Winterbotham, Blakeney and Kirby. Until her death in the 1980s Miss Keymer kept up a keen interest in College affairs, presenting the chapel with a handsome lectern in 1979.

Her successor was Miss Betty Medd from Bristol. As a State Registered Nurse the new Principal had extensive experience of child care, midwifery and health visiting. In this sense she represented a departure from the College's previous recruiting policy, which had favoured administrators rather than the nursing profession for over 30 years. Of equal importance was Miss Medd's valuable experience of the state nursery training sector; she had

Comfort.

worked for 14 years as a health studies tutor in a local authority college running N.N.E.B. courses.

Norland entered the 1970s with 70 students on the roll. The cost of moving from Chislehurst had hit finances to an extent that was still evident; investment was required to upgrade the standard of accommodation and equipment. However Douglas Clarke had warned the board that the College was still running at a substantial loss. There was both an urgent need to generate more income, and a general lack of resources with which to attract it.

Norland's biggest asset was space, which at this time was underutilised. In the Spring of 1970 a report commissioned from a management consultancy included suggestions that might make fuller use of spare beds. A readjustment of the training programme was recommended. The College's most urgent need was, however, for more students.

The curriculum, predictably, came under close examination. At the beginning of Miss Medd's period of office, students spent less than two days a week in lectures; the bulk of their time was devoted to work in the Nurseries and a disproportionate amount of practical housewifery, including laundry for the entire establishment. Under Miss Medd lecturing hours were doubled and, later, redoubled to increase the academic content of the course; subjects such as child development and sociology became cornerstones of the syllabus.

Handicraft, however, remained an important element of the course and nurses were still expected to turn out a creditable piece of smocking. This particular accomplishment has often been spotlighted as an example of Norland's adherence to outdated tradition, but needlecraft was in fact only one of many forms of handiwork. Students also learned basic carpentry and how to make simple musical instruments.

The N.N.E.B. syllabus was constantly evolving, and Norland was obliged to accommodate its changing requirements. A General Studies course was prescribed during the 1970s, and Norland's Tutor, Dorothy Fawkes, devised a syllabus of English, art and music. It was also felt that students should gain a wider insight into practical matters of business, finance and property, all of which impinged upon the conditions that they were likely to encounter in employment.

The strain on the teaching staff was considerable. Funds did not yet run to expansion, and Mrs. Fawkes was obliged to wear a variety of hats. Outside help was recruited in the form of visiting speakers such as estate agents and bank managers. Other extra-mural contributors included a ballet teacher to run music and movement classes, and a health studies lecturer from Reading Technical College.

Practical experience still centred upon the expanding Nurseries, and the rather more fluctuating situation in the Nursery School. To supplement this, students were dispatched to local nursery and infant schools. In any case the N.N.E.B. syllabus required students to learn about the care of five-to-seven year olds, a group which was not catered for within the College operation. Liaison with the local community nursing service enabled students to accompany health visitors and midwives on their home visit rounds. For a short time students were sent into local families (on a non-residential basis) for practical child care work, but this was discontinued because it was felt that the quality of the experience gained was too variable. Whilst they were still learning it was felt that students should practise only in controlled situations. The final hospital term continued to be the consolidating feature of practical coursework, after which graduates went out into their first probationary post.

In the early 1970s Norland students were taking three examinations at the end of their five terms. The N.N.E.B. examination supplied the basic qualification without which no nursery nurse would be recognised by the state. The Norland paper topped this up (it was considered to be of a slightly higher standard), equipping the Norlander with proof of her qualification at what continued to be regarded as the country's foremost training establishment. Finally, many students also opted to take the Royal Society of Health examination in nursery nursing, which was confined to the private training colleges and had, before state regulation, carried authoritative weight with private employers.

Miss Medd felt this to be an unreasonable burden for students, and abolished the R.S.H. examination requirement. The Norland

Jubilee 1977. Lady Atkinson plants a tree.

examination was modified to form a programme of stringent coursework assessment.

Under this new regime the College changed markedly. There was obviously a generally increased level of study and also a less chilly atmosphere. Staff and students enjoyed more informal relations; the nurses found Miss Medd an approachable and sympathetic character. Rules on dress were relaxed slightly; a modest touch of makeup was now permitted and the archaic regulation prescribing hat and gloves, even whilst playing in the sandpit, was modified. Maidens enjoyed less arduous working hours and they were, for the first time, encouraged to spend their free time in the Nurseries playing with the children; hitherto they had been allowed no contact with the babies until they had embarked on their formal course of study.

The social life of the students continued to be a concern, since car ownership was still the exception among their numbers. Links with nearby groups and other educational institutions put Norland on the mailing list of the local social calendar. Students were also encouraged to go to evening classes in Hungerford and Newbury.

Wide-ranging changes were reshaping the theory content of the training programme, but the practical side was also undergoing something of a revolution. Miss Medd wanted to spread the social mix in the Nurseries. Previously, children placed at Norland had tended to come from privileged backgrounds, but they were now joined by needy and handicapped babies from local authorities (who found that Norland fees compared favourably with the cost of care in their own children's homes). Norland thus embarked upon a new social role.

Some of the newcomers were physically or mentally handicapped. There were babies with severe internal disorders, and toddlers with motor difficulty. Others had impaired vision or hearing, but provided that they did not need medical care Norland was happy to offer them a home. One heart-warming success story concerned a baby so severely handicapped that she was diagnosed upon arrival as being without hope of any kind of normal perceptions or reactions. Several years in Norland's intensive nursery care endeared her to all, and her potential blossomed; she was a regular subject of news in the magazine, which eventually reported her happy transfer to a school for the deaf, from which she was adopted.

Social workers initiated the process of finding foster parents and adoptive homes for these children; but the College was closely involved in the selection process, having the most intimate knowledge of each child's needs. Television began to be used to publicise those less easily placed, and Norland took part in several programmes which appealed for prospective parents to come forward. Two German children with Down's syndrome and a visually-handicapped boy were fostered from the Nurseries as a result of the 'Find Me a Family' programme, made with Norland's participation.

Children in local authority care tended to stay for longer than the private placements that had once been the Nurseries' mainstay. Within a year of her arrival Miss Medd introduced the concept of 'families' for these children, creating small groups which could provide emotional and physical shelter from the hurly-burly of the general nursery. In this sense Miss Medd was harking back to the Nurseries of No.11 Pembridge Square, where the separately-named rooms of Dawn and Bluebell created similar cocoons of security. John Burkinshaw, who experienced this as a child resident during the First World War, had commented upon its absence when he renewed his contact with the College as a director at Chislehurst in the late 1940s, but by the 1970s the primacy of the child's interest had been restored, and the system modified accordingly. Each family group had a long-term Group Mother, under whom probationers worked on a one-to-one basis with the children. Continuity of care was the linchpin of the system.

The logical application of this philosophy required year-round provision and, accordingly, the Nurseries remained open over Christmas for the first time in 1972. The practice continued for several years, much to the festive enjoyment of all who chose to stay over.

The Nursery School prospered alongside the expanding Nurseries. By 1973 it was filled to capacity with 55 children on the roll. However its hours were tailored to the school day and calendar, and did not meet the needs of working mothers, who

Family Group.

were becoming the dominant influence in the market for child care services. Day-care was needed: an 8 a.m. to 6 p.m., year-round service that catered for all ages, providing both the stimulus of nursery school work for those old enough, backed up by the cuddles and comforts which are needed by children away from their parents for a longer day. Accommodation for this expansion was carved out within an erstwhile pram store (Miss Medd became for renowned for converting a succession of pram stores to more intensive use) and the Day-Care Unit opened in mid-1975.

By this time the long-term local authority children (of whom only a minority were physically handicapped) outnumbered the private placements in the Nurseries. Those over five were being bussed to and from local primary schools. These children looked upon Norland as home, and Miss Medd was often addressed as Granny. (One child, on overhearing her lament at the insufficiency of cash for some purchase, suggested "Granny, have you thought of getting a job?")

It was apparent that sensitive provision needed to be made for the reunification of families which had experienced long separation, or indeed for children going into foster care after a prolonged period at Norland. Miss Medd was concerned that such new relationships should be successfully established before the child left Norland. The directors consented to Miss Medd's proposal that accommodation should be made available to mothers who needed time and space to bond with their children under such circumstances. Thus the pressures on accommodation were increased, and another pram store yielded.

Whilst Miss Medd invariably placed the interests of the children at the centre of her work, the change in the character of the Nurseries undoubtedly benefited the training programme. Students responded to the challenge of caring for deprived and physically handicapped children, often competing for such responsibility in preference to a less demanding, able-bodied child.

The appointment of a Bursar shortly after the move to Denford had to some extent released the Principal from the onerous duties of financial management. Good housekeeping paid off and a small profit accrued in 1976. Student applications were on the upturn and a stable block was converted for their accommodation. The directors now felt that it was safe to reinstate the third 'O' level requirement that had been dropped when applicant numbers were low.

With so much innovation in hand Miss Medd had little time to devote to the business aspect of Norland's operation. She had undertaken an enormous programme of change, carried through largely on her own initiative because, at this time, the board of directors had become somewhat remote from the day-to-day problems and practicalities. Eventually the burden became too much, and in the summer of 1979 Miss Medd became ill. On medical advice she withdrew from the source of strain and returned to Bristol. For several difficult months the College operated without a Principal (there was no Vice Principal at the time). Lady Atkinson, Vice-Chairman of the board who lived locally in Silchester, was fortunately able and willing to stand in as a co-ordinating and controlling figure on whom the senior staff of the College could lean as they took over the full management of their respective departments during the interregnum.

Chapter Sixteen

THE RECENT PAST

Louise Davison who took up the post of Principal in April 1980 arrived with a formidable battery of academic and career achievements, making her Norland's most highly qualified recruit to date. Trained as a State Registered Nurse at Charing Cross Hospital, she subsequently took a Diploma in Health Education and a Master of Philosophy degree in Health and Human Behaviour at Leeds University. At the time the Norland post was advertised she was lecturing on health education at Leeds Polytechnic, and was chosen from a short-list of 12. This had in turn been whittled down from more than 100 applications, far more potential candidates than the board had ever had to choose from before. Among these were a number of highly qualified staff from competitive institutions - Norland clearly still represented the leading edge of the profession.

At 29 Mrs. Davison was younger than any previous Principal since Miss Sharman. In contrast with her predecessors, all of whom had been unmarried, she was also widowed with a young child. However, within two years she married Christopher Davis a medical officer in the Royal Navy, becoming Mrs. Davis and thereafter, whilst in office, she had three more children.

Thus for the first time the College was headed by a Principal with first-hand experience of running a family, both as a wife and as a single parent. Today Mrs. Davis affirms that the bulwark of an understanding and committed husband, with whom she can share problems, has strengthened her in the professional role, and gives her an advantage which was denied to earlier Principals.

Furthermore, Mrs. Davis is a seasoned Norland employer; she knows in first-hand detail the difficulties that can beset a professional nurse and a working mother needing to build a balanced relationship. Such experience has enabled her to assess the employment conditions and career prospects of nurses with practical insight.

In 1980 the College had by no means risen above the doldrums which had beset its financial health since the move from Chislehurst. A decade of reform under Miss Medd had instituted many beneficial changes and improvements, but the brief period of profitable trading in the mid-1970s had not been sustained. Meanwhile the market for child care was poised for revolution. Legislation in the field of maternity rights was bringing a flood of mothers back to work; their need for child care support was to reshape the profession's prospects out of all recognition.

Demand for student places was buoyant in 1980, but Norland's admissions were limited by residential accommodation and staffing levels. The first task of the new Principal was to introduce an investment programme which would permit the expansion which was clearly needed. Louise Davis had not in fact been chosen for her financial management skills, which in 1980 were untried, but these were to prove a valuable strength in collaboration with the business expertise of the board; the combination was to rescue Norland from economic vulnerability.

The main source of income - tuition fees - had lagged behind inflation because the directors had been fearful of losing potential students to the state sector. The opportunity to bring fees back into line arose with rising unemployment and a fortuitous bulge in applications spawned by the tribulations of the teaching profession. Poor pay, union disputes and low professional morale turned many potential teachers away from the schoolroom and into the nursery. Norland was one of the beneficiaries. In addition

Mrs. Louise Davis.

to this, the TV screening of Wendy Craig's series 'Nanny', though set in the 1930s, brought the profession into higher profile, and prompted an upturn in applications. During the period 1982-85 it was quite normal for applicants to wait a year for an interview.

Mrs. Davis extended the course from five to six terms, in line with N.N.E.B. requirements, and the fees were unflinchingly raised to a level that would ensure solvency. Critics of the fees should perhaps remember that no individual or corporate body takes profit out of Norland; Mrs. Ward's wish that no-one other than the nurses should benefit from her work still endures. It was also her intention that Norland should function as a self-sufficient business, and this too has been sustained although there have been times when the tax exemptions of charity status seemed alluring. The majority of directors have consistently rejected this option, however, on the grounds that such a move would freeze the College's operation within charity law, and could block future expansion and diversification.

The unusual formulation of Norland's articles of association might well merit study by students of economics. There can be few comparable examples of trading success that depend neither on the motivation of personal gain, nor on charitable idealism.

Mrs. Davis inherited a relationship between Principal and board that was not working to the College's best advantage. The life-saving intervention of Douglas Clarke and Lady Atkinson during Miss Medd's absence brought these two directors into close contact with everyday operations, and their experience was to prove a helpful support to the new Principal. But, in general, the board was accustomed to a remote and rather leisurely control. Mrs. Davis confronted her directors with some of the harsher realities of the College's operation, and there was conflict on a number of issues; on such occasions the Principal's view usually prevailed, and the College emerged as a leaner, fitter organisation. It is perhaps noteworthy that today's board contains no survivors from 1980, and that Mrs. Davis was herself invited to join the board in1991, becoming the first Principal to do so.

Mrs. Davis introduced curriculum adjustments, which brought the theoretical content of the course up to the same level as the practical element. The hospital term was switched from the end to the middle of the course, enabling subsequent studies to build upon its input. Students found the change an advantage, because it equipped them with practical experience with which to undertake nursery responsibilities in their second year.

In the lecture timetable greater emphasis was placed on social studies and health education, and Mrs. Fawkes now headed a substantial body of tutorial staff. New subjects edged out the more archaic arts, such as pram cleaning. As computers became standard items of home and nursery school equipment computer studies were introduced as a standard feature of the course.

The Nurseries were experiencing a falling-off in local authority placements because social workers now favoured fostering rather than institutional child care. Most of Norland's children were now short-term residents and Mrs. Davis has been anxious to promote this 'baby hotel' function rather than to allow the Nurseries to become a surrogate home, particularly - as had sometimes been the case in the past - to the unwanted children of wealthy parents. Fresh in the minds of longer serving staff was the case of one such 'poor little rich girl' in the 1970s, who spent almost her entire childhood at Norland until the age of six. Her parents dispatched expensive gifts by limousine from London for each birthday, yet were unwilling to make the journey themselves. Quite apart from the morality of accepting such placements, they often proved to be bad business practice; it was by no means unknown for parents to dump their children in the Nurseries and disappear abroad without paying the fees.

The switch to short-term care was not an easy decision; a refusal to stand in for feckless parents raises the unpleasant question of what alternative care - or lack of it - the child might experience. This is the central dilemma which has faced the Norland Nurseries since the days of Mrs. Dickie, and tends to be overlooked by those who accuse Norland of pandering to the self-indulgence of rich, lazy parents.

However, Norland's role within the sphere of social work, though diminished, was not totally extinguished. Local authorities still depended upon the Nurseries; an emergency call to Norland often saved the splitting up of a family group whose parent had been taken into custody. Norland also continued to play its part in the

135

Speedwell.

care of children prior to fostering and adoption.

The changed character of the Nurseries reduced its demand for student time; more flexible timetabling was possible with short-stay visitors, who did not have the same urgent need for the long-term commitment of one, familiar nurse. Whereas second-year students at one time had to return to the Nurseries after a day of lectures, their weeks were now divided into study days and practical days.

In 1980 there were still many students billeted in seven-bed dormitories, although Miss Medd's conversion of the stable had provided four-bed accommodation for second-year students. Mrs. Davis's determination to improve conditions still further resulted in the opening of a new and separate building, Speedwell House, in 1988. Here, second-year students could relish the unaccustomed luxury of twin rooms. The 10.30 p.m. curfew which had guillotined their social lives in the past now yielded to a system of pass keys, whereby nurses could come and go as they pleased.

As mothers returned to work in ever-increasing numbers the

Primrose Baby Unit.

College's child care operations developed unprecedented waiting lists. The Day Care Unit developed a backlog of 90 applicants; entrants progressed in a continuous stream to the Nursery School, thus mopping up capacity in advance and making entry difficult for newcomers. In Mrs. Davis's development plan, expansion of these facilities became a priority for the 1980s.

In 1989 the Primrose Baby Unit opened, caring for 15 babies aged between six weeks and 12 months. From here the children progress to the Daffodil Nursery (one to two year olds) and thence to Bluebell (two to threes). Thereafter the children enter the Nursery School, where an Extended Day Class separates them from those attending only the shorter, conventional nursery school day. This system recognises that children away from their parents from perhaps nine a.m. until six p.m. need a more cosseted atmosphere, with rest periods and less emphasis on the development of self-sufficiency.

With its unparalleled child care facilities Norland was an ideal workplace for mothers; such a boon should have been a major attraction to staff. Yet, curiously, this was not exploited until the early 1970s when Mrs. Fawkes had her fifth child. A day placement in the Nurseries was an obvious and sensible alternative to losing a vital member of staff. Since then the staff crèche has evolved as a separate offshoot of the Nurseries and, predictably, staff recruitment has rarely been a problem. Mrs. Davis herself has had three more children without slackening the reins of office, and is thus testimony to the fact that a large family need be no bar to high achievement if the appropriate child care facilities are available.

The 1980s were a decade of concentrated media attention upon Norland. Sporadic coverage in the 1970s had included the BBC 'Man Alive' programme focussing on 'Who Will Be Mother?' and an ATV interview with two Norlanders after the birth of Princess Anne's baby. (They were displeased to be addressed as 'Nanny', and to find that interest revolved around trivia rather than serious interest in their training.) However the breakthrough to high profile came with the Wendy Craig serial 'Nanny' shown in the early 1980s, resulting in a surge of enquiries. Norland was not specifically mentioned but Denford suffered an invasion of camera crews

In the pool.

On the swing.

In loving arms.

wanting to compare the modern-day reality with the fictionalised view of the 1930s.

A year later Central TV screened a documentary 'Thoroughly Modern Nannies' which was favourably received, although it concentrated on glamour posts rather than any serious view of training content. TV critics considered the programme to have been "insufficiently hostile".

In 1988 the College featured as a touchdown point for Annabel Croft's helicopter in the 'Treasure Hunt' series. The arrangement had been a closely guarded secret for 16 months, with students being informed only the day before. And early in 1990, Sir Jimmy Savile 'Fixed It' for a 10-year-old to spend a day, courtesy of Norland, as nanny to Mrs. Davis's most recent addition to the family, the three-month-old Harry.

Chapter Seventeen

TODAY
AND TOMORROW

Visitors to Norland today approach via a long driveway from the
A4 through elegant parkland, passing around the eastern side of
the Georgian house. This, unfortunately, incorporates some of the
less attractive extensions built during the nuns' tenure. One
addition, the Principal's house until 1989, now accommodates the
new Primrose Baby Unit. Also on this side of the building is the
Nursery School.

Sweeping around to the north-facing front, the visitor may
appreciate the grandeur of the original architectural concept with
its imposing semi-circular porch borne on paired Tuscan columns.
Evidence of the convent heritage survives in the Angelus bell, the
Madonna statue in its niche, and the stone cross presented by His
Holiness Pope John XXIII. Car parking requirements have
somewhat compromised the spacious effect that was originally
intended, but the lawns have not been sacrificed to vehicles; they
have been dedicated to children, and a variety of playground areas
are dotted around the house.

Inside, the visitor is received into a large entrance hall that has
changed little from its original concept. Stone stairs sweep
majestically up to lecture rooms and library. A passageway to the

right leads through the student common room into the Nurseries and Day Care rooms. To the left, a corridor passes offices and leads down beyond the dining hall towards the Nursery School rooms. On both floors many of the rooms are still characterised by their eighteenth-century proportions and aspect. In the heart of the building the nuns' chapel is now less frequently used than it once was, but nevertheless has been recently refurbished.

There is an initially disorienting variety of passageways and staircases, but the children, both resident and visiting, remain unaware of the rabbit warren scale of the full layout. They are organised and cared for in small groups of like ages, each in its own self-contained suite, designed for a particular style of occupancy. Economies of scale have deliberately not been sought; the babies who come for the day are not, for example, fed from the same milk kitchen that serves babies in the residential Nurseries.

Children who come to these Nurseries tend to settle quickly, thanks to a tolerant policy of tailoring the day (and night) to whatever routine is familiar. Toddlers who at home are accustomed to a long daytime nap and a comparatively late bedtime will not be expected to tuck down at 6 p.m. Meals too are prepared according to the child's home preferences, as far as possible. Each young resident is allocated to the one-to-one care of two second-year nurses, who alternate sharing the infant's routine night and day.

The Nurseries exist to teach students what is best and most up to date in nursery practice. The Matron (who lives on the premises) maintains a close liaison with the educational staff to ensure that new theories gain acceptance simultaneously in the classrooms and in the Nurseries.

The average stay is now only two or three weeks, often while parents enjoy a child-free holiday. The Nurseries also offer a valuable service to post-natal parents at their wits' end with a sleepless baby; whilst a night or two in the Norland Nurseries may not cure the problem, it at least allows the parents to rest and relax before resuming the pressure .

Other placements may be determined by working schedules; Norland is popular with airline crew who work for short periods abroad. Many children visit on a regular basis. Local authorities still make occasional use of the facility for brief respite care.

Making the most of Norland Day Care.

A peaceful setting in Denford Park.

In the new Primrose Baby Unit of the Day Care operation infants tumble and crawl comfortably on a soft green rug spread in front of low-silled, south facing windows. The older Day Care children play in large, sunny rooms generously strewn with the toys appropriate to their age. Most of them attend because parents are working, but a few only-children perhaps, or those who have no easy access to friends of their own age come to benefit from the social experience.

Future expansion will almost certainly focus on this area, creating new groups that will provide for the needs of particular age groups. At present there is concern that the expanded Day Care population is gobbling up too great a proportion of the Nursery School places, leaving reduced opportunity for newly-arrived three-year olds.

Norland cannot hope to provide more than a tiny proportion of the day care places needed even for a relatively thinly populated district like West Berkshire. The area has recently sprouted a number of new private nurseries, crèches and nursery schools. Such is the demand that most have waiting lists. Employers wishing to recruit from the ranks of motherhood are for the first time taking a serious interest in the provision of workplace child care, and many have sought Norland's advice on where to begin. Whilst this has generated opportunities for consultancy on an individual company basis, it has also indicated a more widespread need for a new kind of nursery nurse, who could take on responsibility in industry. The College has recently planned a three-month Nursery Management Course, intended to equip experienced N.N.E.B. graduates with supplementary business, social and legal expertise necessary for setting up and running workplace nurseries.

Today, the girls who enter Norland embark on a six-term course of study spanning two years, including six weeks working in hospital wards. At the end of this period they take first the Norland exam, which is informally viewed as a mock final, before they face the N.N.E.B. papers. The vast majority pass both exams. After nine months' satisfactory performance in a probationary post they are awarded the Norland Diploma.

The student workload is as heavy as it has ever been, although the emphasis is now more on study and less on practical chores. Although the entry requirement asks for only three GCSEs (at Grade C or above), many girls come equipped with A levels. It galls them to find their undergraduate peers imagine the Norland training to be a soft option, involving little more than looking smart with a well-bred baby on one hip. In their second-year, the practical stint in the residential Nurseries (now known as 'The Children's Hotel') requires them to 'sleep in' with their charges, and deal with whatever disturbances may occur during the night. This may mean a nurse could find herself faced with a full day of lectures after the kind of night that leaves experienced mothers pale and harassed. Holidays are minimal by comparison with most colleges and universities.

One of the most arduous academic tasks facing students is the completion of 74 'observations'. Each involves the study of a baby or child in the course of some everyday routine, and noting reaction. The curriculum requires these to be spread over such subjects as social studies, health, education, group behaviour, and environmental studies. Typically one such observation might focus on the way a three-year-old sets about trying to reach a toy on a high shelf - the effort and knowledge that the child displays in the various methods employed to reach or knock the toy down, the point at which help is sought or temper lost. Each of these studies must be written up for assessment; there can be a strong temptation to fall behind with the quota, such that the second year can become dominated by the backlog.

In the area of craftwork students must, in their spare time, produce a wooden toy, a knitted garment, a fancy dress from scrap, a rag doll, a mobile, an educational toy, a sampler book, a wall-hanging and a piece of smocking. Today's students tend to be less accomplished needlewomen than their predecessors; many arrive with no idea how to knit, but all Norlanders can knit by the time they leave. In computer literacy, however, many students arrive with skills not far behind those of their tutors.

The hospital secondment is enjoyed by the students as an opportunity to gain valuable experience in the care of sick children and the newborn in general hospitals and maternity units.

Interviews usually take place at the age of 16 years, after the

An elegant setting for a lecture.

requisite G.C.S.E. passes have been secured. However, entry is deferred until the student is 18, so many spend a year in work before coming to Norland. Others may take a language or cookery course, or complete A level studies.

The vast majority of applications come from teenage girls in this country; a few come from mature women, and there is a small though regular flow of students from abroad. Every application is considered on its individual merits. Open days at the College are held each term, enabling prospective students to see at first hand what the training involves, and to talk informally with current students.

Amongst many legacies of the original Norland Institute, three charitable funds survive to help those associated with the College.

Computer Studies with Dr. Rodney Cox, Vice Principal.

The Isabel Sharman Memorial Fund, set up after the death of the first Principal, is dedicated to helping students who run into financial difficulties in their last year of training. The Emily J. Ward Fund was created to provide recuperative holidays for older Norland nurses. The oldest fund, however, and the one with the widest remit, was set up in the Institute's earliest days; the Norland Benevolent Fund exists to relieve distress for anyone connected with the College.

All three funds are actively managed and used today. Their trustees are often retired directors. Charity law restricts the alteration of a charitable purpose, and today donations tend to be channelled towards the more general Norland Benevolent Fund, enabling the trustees to widen the scope of relief that they can offer.

Each new Principal has made her mark in some alteration to Norland uniform. In Mrs. Davis's case, it has been the jettisoning of the candy-striped overalls worn by new students; all now wear the same fawn dress and chocolate-coloured coat. First and second-year students are distinguished by their collars and belts.

Uniform is nowadays a concern only for students and those in probationary posts (where it is still compulsory). Few modern employers want their nannies in uniform; indeed, those who demand it are often suspected of being more concerned with the social cachet of having a Norlander than with choosing the right personality to care for their children. There is a celebrated instance in Norland folklore of an enquiry to the College for the hire of a uniform - without contents - for photographic use at a christening. Such impersonation is however a rarity. Uniform supply is controlled by Harrods, and orders must be substantiated by proof of eligibility.

In or out of uniform, Norlanders are still highly prized in the vastly expanding job market, where the certificated nurse may be able to choose from up to 20 vacancies. The Registry department created by Mrs. Ward in the early days of the College still operates as a flourishing international employment agency. Graduates of the course must obtain their first, probationary post from the Registry's list of approved employers; thereafter they may find their own work, but the Registry aims to cultivate a strong relationship with nurses in their student days, such that they return throughout their subsequent careers to use the Norland office for appointments and guidance. The Registrar's task has a substantial element of pastoral care; a nurse in trouble or conflict with her employer will usually ring in, confident of practical help and sympathy.

The Registry has traditionally concentrated on vacancies in private families, although it now carries an increasing number of job opportunities in day care nurseries, schools and hospitals. Many Norlanders will typically take a couple of private posts through the Registry before branching out into teaching, nursing or social work. Some will eventually start their own nurseries. Two to three years is now the average in one post, but temporary work has also been a feature of the Registry's service.

The marriage rate among Norlanders is of late very much higher than before; the dedicated spinster nanny is now much less in evidence. Nursery work may continue after marriage in the form of nine-to-five nannying for families who prefer the privacy of non-residential help, and who wish to take full child care responsibility on coming home from work. In some cases this can be a shared arrangement between families.

Once qualified, a Norlander can retire and return to work almost at will. During the Gulf War some, whose husbands were absent abroad, returned to take up temporary work for the duration.

There is still a small market in foreign glamour jobs. Royal families are not as numerous as they were, but their place has to some extent been taken by international celebrities. Here a longer term commitment may be expected from nurses, and elevated social status is not always reflected in an elevated salary. An informal 'top nanny net' circulates information on such posts; news of perks and problems associated with particular employers gets around with commendable efficiency.

The Registry sets out recommended terms and conditions for the engagement of nurses, including minimum salary and free time, and a specific prohibition on employers asking Norlanders to use smacking as a punishment. These terms are used by many as a basis for individual employment contracts. Such formalities are essential, even in the most apparently congenial post where the nurse is expected to be one of the family. There are still some employers who regard income tax and National Insurance as irrelevant trivia in the context of a friendly and casual working relationship; nurses who consent to this do so at their peril.

The press regularly turns up stories of nannies (usually unqualified) who have drifted into jobs without contracts and find themselves working excessive hours at general household chores, in addition to child-minding. Likewise, employers may report horror stories of nannies who drain the drinks' cupboard or run up horrendous telephone bills. Thanks to the formalities of the Registry procedure such disasters are rare in Norland circles, but it is recognised that both employer and prospective nurse may oversell themselves and induce unrealistic expectations at the interview stage; hence the need for firm ground on which to

The modern employer.

establish the appointment.

If Mrs. Ward were to visit Denford today she might query one or two details of the present curriculum but she would certainly approve of her students being worked harder than many of their student peers. The survival of smocking as a carefully preserved accomplishment might please her, but as a committed modernist she would also surely endorse the students' acquisition of computer skills. It might be a disappointment to learn that Norlanders have yet to take up flying lessons, but she would no doubt find traces of 'Slojd' influence in the creative woodwork that students still turn out for their course assessments.

Mrs. Ward would be gratified to note the thriving success of the Maiden scheme, virtually in the same form in which it was originally devised (bar the substitution of Christian names). Whilst paediatric theory has undergone many changes (through Truby King, Benjamin Spock, John Bowlby and Hugh Jolly) she would be unsurprised by Norland's steadfast adherence to the principles of upbringing by loving guidance, never resorting to the heavy hand. In fact her advice on many matters, from breast-feeding to bed-wetting, would not sound dated today.

Mrs. Ward might be mildly astonished at the arithmetic of inflation, which has transformed the tens of pounds per year of her day into hundreds of pounds per week today - both in training fees and salaries. In the matter of the former, Norland still heads the league table of three private colleges by a hefty premium, and an undiminishing stream of student applications testifies to the excellence which warrants it.

Working conditions have perhaps changed most of all. Today's typical Norlander may have entered the College cherishing dreams of an exotic posting with an aristocratic family abroad, but she is more likely, at the end of her training, to opt for a London assignment with a dual-income family that will treat her as one of their own.

Mrs. Ward advised her graduates to position their silver-backed hairbrushes prominently in their new quarters, to ensure that lesser domestic staff understood that they came from genteel origins. Today's employers might run to a daily cleaner, but the display will not be needed. There will be no night nursery separated from the day nursery, but the Norlander will have a comfortable room of her own with a television. Her employers will almost certainly expect her to use the family car, or possibly even provide one for her own use. Whatever the provisions, she will enjoy the protection of a signed employment contract, a copy of which will have been lodged with Norland. The days when such terms and conditions were left to the honour of employers and the thinly-spread vigilance of Mrs. Ward have long since passed.

"I certainly had no free time, set or otherwise. If I was to have a few hours off it took such arranging and was usually cancelled. I did not get to church once in five or six weeks. I often did not have a holiday but took my children home

153

with me, and I never received more than £40 per annum. Yet how happy I was, how perfectly and blissfully content and happy! Though now I realise how selfishly I was treated. I am still in close contact with my children, one of them a grandfather".

Kate Fraser, writing in 1961 of her experiences in Edwardian times.

Above all, Mrs. Ward would be delighted to know that her Institute, now The Norland College, continues to be revered around the world as the pinnacle of achievement in the training of nursery nurses. Around 7,000 nurses pass the N.N.E.B. exams every year, the vast majority of whom attend one of 200 state-financed courses; only 75 are Norlanders. The state-supported students may well regard Norland as a symbol of unabashed elitism, but they would not be in the comfortable positions that they occupy today, during or after their training, had it not been for the foresight, radicalism and executive capability of Mrs. Ward.

THE END

Penelope Stokes
June 1992

BIBLIOGRAPHY

Norland College archives:
   The *Norland Quarterly* and *The Norlander* magazines 1896 - 1991
   Letters and notebooks of Mrs. Emily Ward
   Nurses' Testimonial Books 1892 - 1951
   Minutes of the Committee of Management and the Board of
   Directors
   Press cutting files
   Photograph files
   Prospectus files
   Other correspondence and miscellaneous items
   'A Century of Nannying' (unpublished dissertation)

'Nursery Nursing as a Career for Girls' by Mrs. Walter Ward.
Good Housekeeping, May 1925 pp. 70 and 104.

'The Years of the Nannies' by Mary Ann Gibbs. Hutchinson, 1954.

'History of Bognor Regis' by G. Young, published by Phillmore,
1983.

'The World's Best Nannies Holidayed at Bognor' by Vanessa Mills.
(*Bognor*) *Observer*, 17 Aug 1989 p.9

'The Rise and the Fall of the British Nanny' by Jonathan Gathorne
Hardy, 1980.

'Not Like Other Girls' by Rosa Carey, 1884.

INDEX

Index